# THE TUESDAY GIRL

A Memoir

TANYA EBY

*The Tuesday Girl*


Printed in the United States of America

First Printing, 2023

# Dedication

To Amy McFadden, who walked these years with me. Literally.

And to S.M. Freedman, who from the opening vignettes of this memoir encouraged me to keep going, even when I didn't want to, because I didn't want to. Here's to making it through.

# NOTE:

This is a true story. It is my story. There are many supporting characters in my story, but since they have their own stories to tell, I've tried to keep their lives private. The supporting characters in this piece will feel real, and at the heart of it, they are, but I have changed many of their personal details, merged friends together, or shifted timelines/ locations/ etc. so they have privacy. In that sense, this is also a piece of fiction.

# Table of Contents

# 1. The Expanse

He's still in bed when I tell him I'm leaving. I'm already dressed. I have to get to work and it's getting light out.

"Don't you work from home?" he asks, smiling.

He's rumpled. His hair a mess. Dark eyes sleepy. His chest has hair flecked with silver. He is more fit than I imagined. He is tangled in the sheets, but not trapped. The sheets on him are liquid.

I can still feel him inside me.

The car keys in my hand are heavy and cold.

"I'll make you coffee," he says and lifts the covers. I turn before I see anything. I'll wait for him in the kitchen.

"How do you take it?" he asks and I'm confused for a second until I realize.

"Cream. No sugar. I can't stand sweet coffee."

He stands there in his boxers and nods. His body moves in slow motion while in my head, I'm already flying out the door, down the driveway, and home where it's safe. I tell myself to breathe. To be here. To be *now*.

There's a lot of silence while the coffee brews. Or rather, morning silence which, now that I think about it, isn't really silence at all. There's birdsong, and I can hear the wind. He left the windows open last night, something that felt raw and dangerous.

He hands me the mug and I don't know what to do with the keys and the mug, or where to sit, how to stand, what to do with my purse, my hands, my legs, or my heart. He takes my keys and purse from me and gently sets them on the counter. "Let's go back to bed," he says.

"I want to...but..." My face is hot. So hot. I should be flying away right now. I wasn't ready for daylight.

"We'll just talk. Drink our coffee. It's morning and we both have all the time we want."

If only that were true.

I want to go and I want to stay. I follow him back to bed, keyless.

"It's good," I say. "The coffee."

"It's Keurig. I just pressed the button."

I nod. There's so much I want to say. So much I want to do.

"Tell me where things are at," he says.

It should be easy to talk about, but it's not. "I filed the papers."

“That's great. It'll be hard, the hardest thing you've ever done. But in a year from now..." He sets his coffee on the bedside table and unfurls his arm, encompassing the sparse room with the open windows. So much space.

"I can't do it," I say. I think of kissing him for the first time, something I've wanted to do for twenty years, in the French restaurant over the salad and bread and cheese we shared, in front of everyone. How he didn't care who saw or was watching and how I didn't care either. It was a moment of pure beauty, of heat and softness, of strength and harmony for once, of what's right. The waiter had been standing there and we didn't know until we drew apart. He looked at the waiter and asked, "How'd I do? On a scale of one to ten?"

The waiter smiled and said, "I'd give it a seven."

Then he looked at me and said, "Good. There's room for improvement."

But I can't do it.

Because I can't.

If I leave, Matthew will take the house and half the money. And because I'm self-employed and invested in my business last year, the bank won't give me a loan to buy him out, I checked. The bank also won't guarantee I can get a mortgage on my own and I'll have to start over again. It's harder for a woman. Because it is. I have two kids from my previous marriage, and one of my kids has a severe anxiety disorder, and change will be hard enough. But change with no money and nowhere to live would be too much for them, and they are just starting high school. I only need to hang in there for a few more years...

So later tonight, I have to say I'm sorry and ask if we can stay together instead.

I unfurl my arms.
I have to leave all this,
the wide expanse
and him,
Oh.
I have to leave him behind.

I don't say any of that. We just sit and drink our coffee as the sun starts to shine in.

"You can do it," he affirms.

We talk of other things until the coffee is cool and bitter, and then he walks me outside and in front of his house where the waking neighborhood can see, he kisses me again. "An eight," he says.

"Eight point five," I say, even though, really, it's closer to a nine.

# 2. Backyard Conversation

"You've got to be kidding me. He wants you to go to counseling?" Erin takes a drag on her cigarette and waves the smoke away. I'm sitting upwind so it wouldn't reach me anyway.

"Yep. Marriage counseling."

"But weren't you already seeing someone?"

We are on her back porch, the one that looks out over her enormous wooded property. There's construction going on behind the trees, but you can't see it. Next year, there will be a subdivision and all this will be lost. But for now, we're looking at trees, the stream. An occasional bird flies near us to get a sunflower seed from the bird feeder. I drink my wine. Full bodied red. The kind I like and Erin keeps on hand for me. It's so luscious it's like I'm chewing it.

"I was seeing someone. A life coach. But Matt didn't like where that ended up."

"Because you asked for a divorce?"

"Yep. So my life coach is out. She was clearly a bad influence."

Erin laughs, but not a real laugh. An irritated one. "We've been in counseling. A few weeks now. In therapy, we're together more than we've been in years. I just fucking miss him, you know?" Her next drag on her cigarette is longer. I can tell she's getting ready to talk and I just need to listen. I didn't even know they were having problems. "It's a bunch of bullshit if you ask me. The counselor said we'd focus on getting the spark back. Getting the spark back, my ass. You know what that is? It's coded language. We all know what 'getting the spark back is' and what it means. It means you open your legs more often, all the time and say, 'here's my vagina. Have at 'er.' Getting the spark back is easy. You just fuck him. He's happy."

I laugh. A real one. I take a big sip.

"So in our last session, I decide, you know what? I'm going to be honest here. I'm going to just tell it like it is. So I do. I say I'm sick of having to micromanage everything. I'm sick of having to give him lists, reminders, scheduling things. If you see a piece of paper on the floor, fucking pick it up. I shouldn't have to remind him to do it. I actually tore a big ol' piece of paper out of a magazine and put it in the middle of our hallway, just to see how long it would take him to pick it up. You know how long?"

"A couple of days?"

"Ha! No! It's still there. It's been weeks. Fucking weeks. Then out of nowhere he starts saying I wanted this house and it's too big and expensive and that wears on him. This house is in my name. It's my mortgage. I pay for it. I wouldn't have gotten a house I couldn't afford. But it bothers him. He says I ride him too hard on things and if I just gave him space and time, he'd get to the things that need to be done. Like, you know, unpacking those boxes downstairs that have been there for two years. So then, get this, the conclusion after all this unhelpful talking is I need to be quiet and give him more space, and somehow, he'll magically fill that space and do the things I need him to do. He won't of course, and what he doesn't get and the counselor doesn't get is it isn't even about that fucking piece of paper in the middle of the hallway. It's about intimacy. About connection. Doing things because you care for someone. Being there. Seeing that they're upset and checking in with them. Caring about them. Having a life that's deeper than just the everyday bullshit. I can have everyday bullshit with anyone. I can have that with the deli dude who slices the ham the way I like it."

We sit and listen to the birds. My heart is like a hummingbird in my chest. Wings fluttering.

She stubs out the cigarette. She only smokes half of one, and only when she's stressed out. "And here's the thing. He's perfectly happy. He really is. If only I hadn't said anything. If only I'd been quiet and not tried to make any changes, then everything would be fine. So, I guess now I need, again, to be quiet, and to work on *adding the spark*. I don't want to add a spark. The last thing I want to do is fuck him. If you want intimacy with me physically, you've got to be intimate with me emotionally. And what truly gets me going is everything in marriage is just a setup to make women stay quiet. Be sweet. Be motherly. Be open and have your vagina ready to go for him. Soothe him. Buoy him up. Fuck that shit."

I take a sip of wine and smile. I agree with her. Of course I do.

Maybe I won't go. Maybe I'll tell Matt he's the one who needs to change. Not me. If I put a piece of paper in the middle of the floor, what would he do? Would he pick it up? I don't think he'd even see it. He'd step right on it. I say softly, "Fuck that shit." Just trying the sentence on. Fuck it.

"You need more wine?" Erin asks.

# 3. Counseling

I'm not sure which is worse: waiting in the attorney's office to go over divorce papers, or sitting next to Matthew now, waiting to head into couples counseling that I don't really want. It's not that I don't believe in counseling, I do. I've had plenty of therapy sessions over the years. I'm just not sure what is broken between Matt and I can be fixed.

Over the last six months of being separated, though, he's done the things I asked. He's started working out, he's seeing friends, he's being active, he's working on his depression. I'm not sure he's really talked to his doctor yet about his antidepressant, but he says he has. When Matt talks to me, it's like he speaks in exclamation marks, and everything sounds fake. "Had a great day at work! Sold so much stuff! Got them to take an upgrade!" He can talk about that, but he can't ask me about my day. He can't really connect with me.

I'm convinced the problem here isn't really me or our relationship. The problem is Matt. It's a chemical problem. Counseling isn't going to help.

We sit in the waiting room. The furniture is faux leather and there are two waterfalls. "Don't you think that's a bit of overkill?" I ask. He looks at me as if he's confused. "So many calming waterfalls."

He smiles, but not really.

In the office, the therapist asks what we want to accomplish. "I'm here because he asked me to come to counseling."

"Okay. But what's your goal?"

She is older than both of us, grandmotherly like, and I think that's a good thing. I want to be completely honest here, but being honest could crush him. "We're here because I wanted to get a divorce and he said if I left him, he would kill himself."

There is silence. I can't even hear the waterfalls in the lobby.

"Matthew," she says gently. "Is that true?"

His face is red. His sorrow trembles right at the surface and I am enraged by it. I want him to tell the truth. To talk about what he's feeling. He doesn't talk about emotions though. He makes jokes. He changes the subject. He avoids. He retreats. He plays on his iPad while I narrate all day, write, pay bills, organize our house, shop, cook, take care of the kids. He doesn't say or do anything.

"Is that true? Do you have a plan to kill yourself?"

"I've done research," he says, and it sounds proud.

"Do you have a plan to do it?" she asks again, and I wonder if there's some magic combination of words he's supposed to use to trigger some kind of action, or intervention, or if we can, I don't know, maybe get him some psychiatric care. I can't care for him anymore. I'm too drained. And I promised myself a long time ago, I would never be on suicide watch for someone again.

I'm angry he's forced me into this position.

"I do not have a plan," he says. "After all my research, I haven't found something that's a sure thing."

It stops my heart a little to hear that. "You haven't killed yourself because you're not sure it would work?" I ask.

"Pretty much."

What I want to have happen now is I want the therapist to tell me to get me and my kids out of this situation. I want her to give me approval to leave. I want her to say the problem isn't our marriage. Our marriage can't be fixed. My husband is so depressed, he wants to die, but he hasn't done it because he's not sure he can be a success at suicide. He's afraid of failing...at suicide.

Every atom in my body is triggered. I am not safe. I am not safe here. I am not safe here with this man.

But the therapist does not give me permission. She continues to talk to him throughout the session, asking about his past, trying to get him to open up, but he won't.

At the end of the session, she says, "I've counseled a lot of couples and the ones who are successful, both want the marriage to succeed. But I have to be honest here...I'm not sure we can even talk about your relationship right now. I'd recommend Matthew meet with another counselor first for some time to explore some of these issues, and then, maybe, we can try this again."

I look at the therapist and try to tell her with my eyes that if she couldn't save my husband, maybe she could save me.

On our way home, Matthew says, "I don't like her. I thought she was really condescending. She's just trying to get more money. Marriage therapy is supposed to focus on the marriage, and it was like she was just attacking me the whole time. She didn't ask you about any of your issues, she just focused on me the whole time."

I don't say anything. What is there to say? It's never about Matthew. It's never his problem. Matthew is fine. Our marriage is fine. So what if we're both miserable, if we just smile and stop trying to talk about things, everything is fine.

That night, though, lying next to him in bed, I'm terrified. What if he finds a foolproof way to kill himself? Will he do it? Will he do it in front of the kids? Will he take me with him?

It feels like I'm being dramatic or hysterical, but the fear I have of him is bone deep. If I leave him, he kills himself. If I stay, I die a little bit more every day.

He rubs my back, tells me goodnight, and rolls over to sleep. I try to sleep, but I can't. The weight of my responsibilities is too heavy to let me rest.

# 4. FRIDAY AFTERNOON

I don't really want to let my mother-in-law, Susan, inside, but I invited her and the therapist said it's going to take time and effort to heal relationships so...

"Have a seat. Can I get you anything to drink? Water? Coffee?"

"I don't want anything," she says, even though I can tell she does.

She sits on our gray couch, and Reggie, our golden pup, splays at her feet.

How do I even begin? I want to talk to her like a woman, like a friend, but she is my husband's mother first. I want to ask her why she wouldn't answer my calls, my texts; why she immediately blocked me on Facebook. Why, knowing her son and his mental health issues over the years, she couldn't imagine that maybe there was a reason I'd have to leave?

It's so hard, sometimes, to talk about the real things when we are trained to pretend they don't exist. *I'm doing well, thanks. Nice morning. Beautiful day today.* But I am tired of all of this so I say, "What do you want to know?"

She's petting the dog right now, looking around the living room, maybe noticing the changes I made while her son was gone. While he lived at their condo when they were still in Florida. He has been back now for over a month, but I haven't changed things back to the way they were. There is more color in the house now. I have a vase of fresh flowers, new plants, new pillows with a floral, girly pattern on them. I've spent years trying to keep the house décor more masculine to suit his tastes. Why didn't I ever decorate to suit mine?

She doesn't say anything for a bit and then, she starts. It is my job to listen. "I don't understand how you could kick him out like that. So, he was a little depressed. If he had cancer, you wouldn't leave him, would you?"

I think, maybe, I would, if Matt wouldn't take his medicine. If he wouldn't get help. If he asked me to take the chemo for him. I move to answer but there is more she wants to say. "A marriage is *work*. It's *hard*. You don't get to make those choices. I've been married almost fifty years and there were times..." There's a hitch in her voice. Reggie rolls over, baring her belly and Susan pets. "I was suicidal twice during my marriage. And you can get over a lot. You can forgive a lot. I forgave Ben for so many things. But that's marriage. That's what you do." She looks at me just for a beat. "You? You have so much more than I did."

I can fill in the blanks here. The things she doesn't say. I have a career. Friends. I have more than just the home and kids and my husband. I have an identity outside of these walls. She's never had a job, or rather, her job has been to raise her three children and take care of her husband. Ben likes to joke that he asked her to marry him because out of all the girls he was dating, she looked the best in a tight sweater.

"You know, one time, I almost left him. I wanted a horse. Not to own, but to rent. We could afford it. I had a friend and I could go to the farm once a week, on the weekend, to ride the horse and take care of it. Tend to the stall. Groom him. Ben had a boat and friends and time away. He had vacations and work trips. I was home alone with the kids. All the time. Every minute. And I just wanted this one thing. Just this one. I told him I'd leave him if he didn't let me have this horse."

"Did he agree?" I ask, hoping for her sake he did. That he'd let her have one thing of her own.

"He said it was a waste of money and I needed to be home with the kids. I got over it. I moved on. It was probably just hormones. I was about your age then. Probably about to go through the change."

"It's not hormones," I say.

Reggie jumps off the couch. The silence is heavy. Susan's hands are in her lap now, clasped together, steady, frozen. "And you know, he was right. It was a foolish thing. What would I do with a horse? I'm too old now, of course, to ride one. But I think about it sometimes. We all give up things in marriage. It's how it is."

I want to know: what did Ben give up?

How do I tell her that all the things that made a marriage good, were absent from mine? My husband's depression affected every aspect of our life together. His moods were up and down. He wouldn't participate in anything. Didn't want to leave the house, or do anything around the house. He spent hours on his iPad, in his office, on the computer. There was no sex. No affection. No conversation. The kids were afraid around him, of his moods, his ups and downs. "I'd never hurt them," he said once, his voice even.

"But you just admitted you want to kill yourself," I said. "That you have a plan." He looked at me like I was the crazy one. "You can hurt someone just by hurting yourself," I wanted to say, but I couldn't. I was too afraid. I thought of the thin line between sanity and madness. All it could take was one wrong word. The real trouble was, you could never know what that one wrong word was, and how, moment to moment, that one word could shift.

It is not a good marriage. There is no love here. Depression eroded any love there was ages ago. Is it enough to leave a marriage because you are unhappy? But it's a wife's duty to stay, even now, in this day and age. A wife *stays.* I know this. And this is what Susan is telling me.

I look at her, perched on my couch. She is a fragile bird, trembling and about to take flight.

She won't hear anything I say to her. In her mind, I'm a traitor and cruel. It's already been decided. If not by her, then by her husband and mine. I'm the kind of woman who would leave her spouse if he was dying of cancer. I'm the kind of woman who puts herself first.

Then I say the one real thing of the entire day. "But, Susan. Imagine if you'd been able to ride that horse? Imagine what your life could've been like if you hadn't stayed? If you'd walked away?"

She doesn't say anything to that.

She asks for a glass of water and I get her one, and then when she is leaving, she tells me she's making kielbasa and sauerkraut on Sunday. My husband's favorite. We are all invited over for dinner.

# 5. Late at Night

We are in bed. The kids are at their dad's house and there was a time, a long time ago, when Matt and I would have used this time to make love, to rediscover each other and what it meant to be two people instead of two parents. But that is not what I'm waiting for tonight.

I wait for Matthew to turn the light off.

Sometimes it's easier in the dark, if I catch him before he picks up his iPad and I pick up my Kindle, and then we both turn on our sides facing away from each other to sleep. If I catch him before all that, maybe I can get at something that's true.

"What did we talk about when we were happy?" I ask.

"Huh?" he asks.

I realize it must seem like a strange question, coming out of nowhere in the dark.

"When we were happy?" I say, as if repeating it helps clarify. "You know, when the kids were four and five. When we were doing things together all the time. What did we talk about then? It seems like we were always talking."

"I imagine we talked about the kids. And anyway, what's this about 'when we were happy'? I thought we were happy now."

It has been almost a year of being back together. Of working toward...something. I don't know what that something is, exactly. It's not the future. We don't talk about the future much.

Our lives are firmly in the now.

"We are happy now," I say.

Now, what we talk about is work, what's happened, what's stressful. Matthew tells me about all of the commissions he's making and all the people who turn to him and ask for help. He tells me about all the times he's right about something. When he talks, he puffs up and I can almost see the peacock feathers unfurl. I tell him about my day. My narration gigs. My workflow. The kids.

We talk a lot about what food we're going to eat. What are you hungry for? Indian? Chinese? Should I make it? Get takeout? How about I draw up a meal plan and you can stop at the store and we'll load up on things?

But then, we just have to talk about food again in a few days.

What we don't talk about is how small our lives are. In our house. In this bed. Our backs to each other.

I think, sometimes, of a great vastness that was before me for a while. I think of a partner who picks up the litter on the floor or who says, yes, take the horse for a ride, and go and go and go. I think of a partner who says, you know, today was shit, and then tells me all the details and the struggles of it.

I think, sometimes, of camping outdoors and staying up by the fire, watching the flames spark and jump. I think of cold kisses under a dark sky and fumbling to get closer to each other for warmth, not just of the body but of the mind.

He reaches for his iPad and turns it on. The room is bathed in a blue glow, but it's all right. I can fall asleep to it.

"I'm having trouble going to sleep," I say. "Can you...can you just tell me something nice? Something that makes you happy?"

"Huh," he says again, thinking. Then he tells me about a podcast he listened to. Not how he felt or what he thought, but he repeats the podcast. He has a good memory for this, telling all the things they covered in the podcast and interesting facts and quotes.

I know I'll drift off to sleep, listening to the sound of his voice, but not catching any of the meaning of his words.

# 6. Sandwiches

I'm making sliders for dinner tonight. It should feel fun, shouldn't it, mini sandwiches for dinner! Appetizers as a full meal! But mostly I just feel lazy. I feel like I'm not doing a good enough job cooking healthy, balanced meals for my kids and husband. There is so much a good mother and wife is supposed to do.

Still, these sandwiches are better than frozen pizza. I've cut the Hawaiian rolls in half, layered them with ham and swiss cheese, and now I'm mixing the butter sauce to pour over the tops of the sandwiches.

I don't even hear my son approach. I just feel him. I look up, the pot with the melted butter sauce in my hand, about to pour.

"Gah!" I say.

"Did I scare you?" My son is fifteen and he seems pretty pleased with the thought that maybe he scared me. He did scare me, but mostly because he has new whiskers on his chin and he grew three inches overnight. When did he change and I am not the mother of a man-boy? How could I be? When did this happen? When did he grow up?

"You did scare me," I say. "Good job."

I pour the butter evenly over the sandwiches. He watches me.

"Steady hand," he says.

"I've had a lot of practice."

"You'd probably be good at gaming if you gave it a try."

"I did give it a try."

"You did? When?" He sits at the counter. Now that we are speaking the same language, he's decided to stay for a bit.

"I used to try to play that Disney game, *Dragon's Lair* or something."

"No way! Like, the old-school arcade one?"

"Yep. I couldn't play it. So I gave all my quarters to your uncle and made him play it for me."

He considers this. "That's the saddest thing I've ever heard."

"Why?" I ask, smiling. "I finally got to see how it ended."

"How did it end?"

"Funny, I can't remember."

He nods knowingly. "Saddest. Thing. Ever."

We listen to the cuckoo clock ticking. I wait. He's here for something. He takes a breath. "Look," he says. "Could you just not look at me for a minute. I just want to say a thing and then I want to go back upstairs and play *Skyrim*."

I nod. Grab the tinfoil and begin to cover the sandwiches with it. While he talks, I work hard not to look at him, and instead focus on sealing the foil around the pan.

"Scarlett and me, we don't understand why you don't just leave him."

At first I want to interrupt him. I didn't even know he and his sister talked. I didn't even know they'd noticed I'd tried to leave Matt. But he doesn't give me time to interrupt. "And I know you're going to say that marriages are work and blah, blah, blah, and all that. I get it. We both do. But we've seen you work. And work. And work. And things aren't getting better. And he's weird, Mom. He's changed. Something is off. Why do you think we're in our rooms all the time? I mean, besides being teenagers and all. Look. You're not happy. I just look at you sometimes and it makes me...mad, you know? And Scarlett and me—we just wanted you to know that you shouldn't stay with him for us. That's, like a bad thing. A really bad thing. And if you're not leaving him because you don't think you can do it, well, you need to know you are stronger than you think you are. And we'll be there. Me and Scarlett. We see how things are. And, yeah, so, I'm going to go play my game. When's dinner?"

"Thirty minutes or so," I say.

Then, he's gone.

The edges of the foil are perfectly crimped. I put the pan in the oven, set the timer, and head into the bathroom because I can't stop shaking.

My kids see me.

# 7. The Storm

It's a blizzard outside, but you wouldn't know it in here. Out the doors, the world is dark and encased in ice. The roads are slick and the trees and power lines click with the ice. It's so cold that when I breathe, the air freezes in front of me, just enough to prove I'm alive.

But inside the small pub, everything is noise and warmth and golden.

Erin and I grab a large table. We're expecting a lot of people to show up. We've scheduled a big get together for local audiobook people to attend: narrators, engineers, producers, and proofers. The restaurant has been informed.

In a half an hour, the place is packed and we've had a round of GG&Ts (ginger, gin & tonics) and the table is littered with drink napkins, small pottery plates, and the first round of appetizers: house-made pickles, deviled eggs, biscuits with hot honey.

There's jazz playing. Something from the '30s. Maybe it's a speakeasy we're in. The bar is trying, but it gets a lot of the details wrong.

I don't hear him come in. There's too much noise for that. But I feel him. A breath of cold wind, a swirl of color, the air sucked out of my lungs. He's wearing a jacket I've never seen before. It makes me sad that I don't know it. I can feel him under me, inside me, my fingers toying with the silver hair on his chest. The snow on his shoulders, in his hair. Immediately, he hangs his jacket on the wall next to where we sit, and shakes hands, laughs, and hugs the people we are both here to see. Colleagues. People we work with all year round but rarely see. It's a meetup that calls us out of our homes and offices. A holiday get-together for the artistic crowd. There will be flash-fried brussels sprouts, pulled pork, and bread pudding. There will be too much money spent, and great joy in doing it. He is happy to be here.

He is so handsome it hurts.

Erin looks at me. "I think you need another drink!" I like that it's not a question. She calls for the waiter and orders another gin drink. Something with fizz.

He doesn't look at me at first. But maybe he feels me too.

There is laughter and conversations drift in the air like the whirling snow outside. I can't focus. I can't discern words. I have a flash of being in his arms, of his lips on my neck.

And then his lips are on my cheek. "Hey," he says and sits. Next to me. The one open seat. How convenient. How tragic.

He looks around. Orders a margarita. On the rocks. With salt. He doesn't care it's a craft cocktail place. He wants what he wants.

What do I say to him? What do I do?

"How are things?" he asks, "With you and the husband? How are the holidays?"

He could say this to anyone. He probably already has. He's smiling and he's saying the words, asking all the right questions, and they don't mean anything, and I don't mean anything when I say, "Oh, good! Things are good! How are things with you?"

He tells me business is good. Things are looking up. He's traveling soon, out west. Going hiking in some remote place. There will be no Wi-Fi. No cell service. Just him and his companions. Three middle-aged men roughing it.

What happens then is hard to describe but it's like a small detonation inside me. My own personal nuclear explosion, inside, unfurling. A bright orange flower of heat and fire so quick and strong it's shocking in its fury.

"I missed you," I say.

"What's that?" he asks. The restaurant is loud and you can't whisper anything. Plates and silverware clang. An iPhone goes off. Someone's singing drunkenly.

"I've missed you!" I say, louder. But I don't stop there. "Things aren't okay! I'm not okay! Something has to change!" I don't care who hears. I'm shouting now. I'm shattering the ice outside that's encased around the fire hydrant, the cars that have been parked for too long.

He doesn't say anything at first. Then the waiter brings him his drink. He licks the edge and then takes a long sip. "I was just coming for a drink," he says. "And then I was going to leave. But maybe is there another menu? I could stay for dinner." He looks at me and I nod. He smiles and continues, "Maybe I'll stay for a while. Maybe I can make some time for a long meal. You know, to celebrate. The season."

***

He kisses me like I'm about to disappear and his kisses are the only things keeping me present. Maybe that's true. We don't talk in the hotel room, not with words. He pulls my shirt off, doesn't even notice the lace bra and immediately undoes the clasps, all while kissing me. I reach for his belt, try to undo it, but I'm fumbling. I've forgotten how to undress someone. Somehow, we manage and it is only seconds before we are standing naked with each other, the moonlight pouring in from the window.

He is so hard I blush, and I thrill a little at being the cause of it. At our age, with my soft belly and wide hips, I thrill at the idea this man can want me so much that his dick stands straight out like some kind of divining rod.

My husband greeted me with softness, even when I worked him with my hands, my lips, my heart. We tried and tried and then we'd give up. The last time, months ago, when we were in bed together, panting and sweaty from our exertion of trying to love each other, he said into the darkness, "I'm sorry. I'm just not attracted to you anymore."

What do you say to that? How do you move on? I think that maybe, I apologized. He was right not to be attracted to me. I'd put on weight over our marriage. I'd aged. My breasts had drooped a bit. What was firm and flat before now had weight to it. I was a terrible person for aging, for 'letting myself go.'

So it was my fault. And it was crushing.

The one person who was supposed to love me forever, couldn't bear to be with me.

But this man.

This man is different.

I am still round and older. I am not a woman in her twenties, I am a woman who is almost fifty, and my body shows the years. My body has earned the years. And he looks at my full breasts, my sloping hips, the untrimmed hair between my legs, and what he sees, what he feels is desire. For me.

I reach for him, for the length of him, for his hardness, for his want.

"In me," I whisper. "Now."

I push him on the bed, filled with an energy to take what I need. To not ask. To not just lie there and accept. To not plead or try to impress or coerce or say, "Look at me, aren't I enough? Aren't I pretty enough?"

No. What I say instead is, "I'm going to fuck you." I kiss him this time, with every ounce of my being. And I straddle him, sink down on top of him, and take him inside me until I am filled with his want. I rock back and forth on him. He reaches for my breasts and I tell him to pinch my nipples so I feel it. I want to feel everything. And I do.

Oh, God, what pleasure this body was made for even at almost fifty. Especially at almost fifty.

For how long have I neglected to give myself this in an effort to be supportive and understanding?

There is no apology here. I am desirable. I am wanted. And for the few moments in the hotel room with the moon spilling over our linked bodies, I am filled. I own it. I own myself.

We climax at the same time. It is a burst of stars, a flash of white light.

I collapse next to him, spent and boneless, panting.

"Holy shit," he breathes and laughs.

I laugh too.

So I say, "When can you go again?"

***

Matthew is up, waiting for me. He's been in the spare room for months now and he lies in bed, his iPad on his chest, the screen illuminating his face in blue. This is how we live now. Blue smiles covering our skulls.

His door is propped open so he can see me when I come up the stairs and cross to what used to be our room.

I pass him and don't say anything. We rarely speak anyway. It's nothing new.

"You were out late," he calls to me and a wave of red-hot rage washes over me.

Now he notices? He notices that I've been absent and am only now returning? What about the years I've been gone, the years I've disappeared from even myself in my effort to serve him, be loving, be supportive, put aside all my needs for him?

I could ignore him. I could go in my room and shut the door, but I don't. Something within me propels me to turn around, to walk to his room, to look at him in bed and say, "Why are you here? I hate you. I hate you. Do you understand? Get the fuck out!"

Then I smile. A real smile. A smile wide and true and terrifying.

This cruelty isn't like me, and it is exactly like me. It's who I've become.

The words are terrible and ugly and I think I hear him crying, but I don't care. I don't care. I don't care.

I go to my room. I shut the door.

I sleep for hours and hours.

# 8. A Thaw

Erin isn't smoking anymore. She's trying to make good life choices. It's made her really hard to be around. She knows this. "I fucking hate being healthy. It's exhausting and it's stupid." We are walking around Reed's Lake. It's four-point-five miles and it might as well be 200 miles. We are terrible at this. "But," she continues between big gasps of breath, "I don't want to die. I'd like to live another few years, at least so I can have sex again."

"You can have sex now," I say.

"With my husband? God no. He's still not getting any. Not until he fixes things in our relationship."

I admire Erin and her complete commitment that everything wrong in her relationship has nothing to do with her. "It's not *me*," she says. "It's fucking *him*. He's being a child. You want to know the one sure way to fuck your marriage up? Turn your wife into your mother. Make your wife your caretaker. That's how."

She's not wrong.

"So you finally did it?" she asks. "You broke it off with him?"

"I did."

"Tell me everything."

I try to think of everything, but it feels like too much, so I just make it simple. "I said terrible things. I told Matt I hated him."

"Is it the truth?"

"Yes." I don't have to think about it.

"Then good. Enough of the bullshitting and tiptoeing. Fucking tell it like it is. I think that's what messes up marriages in the first place. All the tiptoeing. The 'I' statements. When something is wrong, say it. Don't cushion it so you don't hurt their little feelings or, God forbid, threaten them. When they're being a douche, tell them. When they've sucked you dry of every single emotion and you're worn out and you hate them, tell them."

I kind of agree with her, but I also feel horrible. It was a terrible thing to say. And I've become a terrible person. Part of me, though, feels like he deserves it. Why couldn't he just let me go the first time?

"You know what did it?" I ask. Now I'm breathing heavy. The air is crisp. It's one of those peculiar winter thaws that happens in Michigan. Between ice storms and sub-zero weather, we occasionally get a day where the sun comes out, and things sorta melt. It's a balmy thirty-nine degrees, so we're taking advantage of it. It will probably be weeks before we can walk again.

"What?" she asks.

"It's not I told him I hated him. It's not I refused to stop seeing you know who. It's not that our relationship is terrible, that we don't talk, we don't have sex, it's none of those things. He's not leaving because we both agree the relationship is beyond fixing. He agreed to move out because I told him I'd sell the house."

This stops Erin.

But also because she needs a cigarette.

"I'm sorry," she wheezes. "I can't. How long did I last this time?" She checks her watch. "Forty fucking minutes. I'll only smoke half."

We stand a little to the side of the walking path. The trees drip. A runner glides past.

"He agreed to the divorce because you said you'd sell the house?"

"I guess that was the thing. He didn't want me to get the house. He didn't want me to buy him out and keep the house. These two years of misery, of trying to fix things, were just because he wanted money from the house."

"Fucking asshole. The only reason you have that house in the first place is because you bought it. It's in your name, right? You used the money from your old house for the down payment?"

"He couldn't even get on the mortgage. His credit was too bad."

"But he deserves half the house?"

"Michigan law," I say. It's heartbreaking. And with my job and the bad year I've had, I'm not sure I can get a new mortgage. Staying though is worse than the unknown and that is saying something. My kids agree. My kids can see it too.

I can't stay with him anymore.

I can't.

Erin inhales. She smiles. I see the calm rush over her in a gentle wave. She takes two deep drags then stubs the cigarette out onto some ice.

"Fuck," she says. "Now what?"

We start walking again. A little slower this time. Now what, indeed? What happens next? How do we untangle things? Where do I go? Where will the kids and I end up? Will they want to stay with me or live with their dad, husband number one?

Will Matthew kill himself like he's threatened? Will it be my fault? Will I care?

I don't like who I've become.

I'm terrified of who I'm going to be.

"What happens now?" I ask. "Do we just finish this walk?"

"Stupid fucking idea, this walk. Next time I suggest something like this, you just tell me to fuck off."

# 9. Front Porch

After weeks of limbo, it's finally happened. Matt's stuff is gone. The house gutted of his boxes, his mug collection, his photos from college. There's a strange echo in the house and the house feels twice as large now without his presence in the rooms. I can still feel him, but it doesn't scare me. It's just the last chords of a song ending.

I feel like I can breathe again.

The kids are at their dad's and the dogs look at me, confused by the extra space, the silence, the absence.

I call the man I've been seeing on and off. No more need to meet in hotel rooms or at his place. We can spend time here, in my house, which is my house for another three weeks before it becomes someone else's house.

I fantasize about having sex with him in every room, on every available surface, as a way to claim my body, to say I am vibrant and alive, and wanted. See? Look, how much this man wants me, he'll take me on the counter, in the bathroom, in the basement, my bare ass seated on the cool top of the dryer.

Instead, though, he comes in through the back door and peers around the corner. "Holy cow," he says. "It's pretty empty."

I laugh. "That's my life now, I guess."

I look at him and expect him to kiss me, to sweep me into his arms, but he doesn't. It's awkward, this waiting. He shyly hands me a bottle in a brown paper bag. "Cheers," he says. "It's a screw top. I didn't know if he left you a wine opener. When my wife left me, she took everything."

I laugh. Not because it's funny, but because it's painful. I don't have a wine opener either. Or a dining room table. Or bookshelves. Or a life plan. I don't even have a *now* plan.

We open the wine and I pour two coffee mugs full. "I've got Ritz crackers, salami, and some shredded cheddar cheese." It's literally all I have. I don't know how to shop for just myself so I just didn't.

"Perfect," he says.

We take the wine, cheese, and the crackers and go outside to the expansive front porch that Matt and I loved because of all the parties we would have out there. We never did. We just had a wide front porch we never used.

It's still a little cool out, but it's a pretty spring day. We sit on the plastic patio furniture and I try to just be content with what this is, whatever it is.

"You're going to be fine," he says.

I nod.

"You're going to be great. You have so much going for you."

I look at him. He's saying something, but he's meaning something else.

"I can't stay long," he says. "I've got to get home to Julie."

It hits me in the gut. I know in a flash there will be no lovemaking in every room. No more meetings. No more future with this man of passion, trips, laughter, good food, and great sex. Whatever I thought I had with him just went up in smoke.

"Who's Julie? I didn't know you had a Julie." I don't know how my voice sounds. I hope it doesn't sound like grief.

"I didn't have a Julie. Well, I did, but it wasn't really anything, but now...she's just so IN my life now, you know. Our kids go to school together and she hangs out with my mom, takes her to appointments, and she's always in the house and..."

"Do you love her?" I ask. It feels really important.

"Don't ask me that."

What I really want to ask is "Don't you love me?" I thought we had something epic. I thought...I don't know. I thought I was special, but I guess it was something just average. "What about..." My voice quivers and I hate it.

"You're amazing. I hope our time together...I hope I made you feel better."

Then I laugh for real. A big laugh. Bold. Deep. It's that kind of laugh you can't contain. It just bubbles up. It lasts longer than it should.

He looks at me and gives me a half smile and I want to knock the smile off his face.

I could offer him reassurance. Sure, you made me feel better. It was just sex, wasn't it? It wasn't a relationship. We've known each other for thirty years, but it wasn't anything, because I'm not a Julie. Now you have a Julie. You made me feel better, though. You gave me lots of orgasms and after years of feeling like I was nothing, like

I was repulsive, like no man would ever want to be near me, let alone inside me, you made me feel loved.

I don't say that.

I take a deep draw on my mug. Feel the wine go down. "Go home," I say.

***

I sit out on the porch for a long time. Until it gets dark, until the hint of cool in the air becomes full-on freezing. I sprinkle cheese on the ground for the dogs who, at first, are delighted, and then they just want to go inside where it's warm and known.

I sit there.

It's so quiet.

I am so confused. How did I get here? Was this what I wanted? Was it? How do I take this empty life and make it into something amazing? Is it even possible?

I finish the wine. I head inside when I am drunk and numb and I realize there are no answers.

# 10. Romance

I've been an audiobook narrator for almost two decades and most of the titles I record are romances. I wake the kids up, get breakfast going, make lunches, take the kids to school, and then fire up my recording studio in the basement. I grab my hot water, my iPad, my reading glasses, tell the dogs it's time to go to work, and head downstairs to where passion, angst, and happily ever afters await me. I am not immune to the irony. Every day, I spend hours performing books where characters meet and fall in love, overcoming unbelievable odds because their love is so strong, and I can't even find a decent date to get a burger with. Maybe this is why we need romance novels. Not because they tell us how the world is, but because they give us hope for how the world could be.

"How's your schedule this month?" Erin asks me on the phone. We've fallen into the habit of checking in with each other on a daily basis, around ten when I've already been recording for a few hours, and just before Erin is ready to start.

"My schedule is kind of shit," I say. "Honestly, I'm a little scared. There are holes in my recording schedule where there shouldn't be holes."

"Did you send out your emails?"

"I did. To all my clients saying I'm here, I'm available, choose me. Only they're not choosing. And I can't get the big publishers to give me a chance. I just don't understand it. It's like I'm too old or something."

"You're not too old."

"I am! I'm almost fifty, and still reading romances. Who wants to listen to someone who sounds like a mom get it on with a motorcycle club president?"

Erin laughs. "I mean, I kinda do."

"And I don't know what to do to get on the treadmill with Penguin or Hachette or Macmillan. I've recorded almost a thousand books and they still have no interest in me."

"I don't understand it either. Maybe it's because we're in the Midwest and not NYC or LA."

"But you're with some of those publishers," I say. I'm honestly not jealous. I'm just frustrated.

"I know. Like I said, I don't understand it. And you work steadily for people who won't give me the time of day. It's like they actively dislike me."

"No one actively dislikes you," I say. "You're too endearing."

"Well, okay, maybe they reluctantly dislike me." She pauses. "You okay with money?"

"I'm okay. Not great, but not terrified yet. I'll see if I can get a gig from an indie author. I'll post to Twitter, send out a call to the universe, sacrifice a virgin."

"Good luck finding one of those."

"I'm just tired, Erin," I say. "I'm tired of trying so hard all the time. Hustling. Trying to convince people to love me."

"You don't have to convince anyone to love you."

"But I do." Now we're not talking about work or gigs. Now we're talking about my heart. Why my dad didn't want to be in my life, why Matthew didn't love me enough to want me, why depression was more attractive than working on things, why a man I felt passion for felt more passion for this Julie instead.

"I love you," Erin said. "You didn't have to convince me."

"No. You arm-wrestled me into being my friend. And I love you too."

"Too bad we're not lesbians."

"I'm not convinced lesbians have it any easier."

"No," Erin agrees. "But they probably have way better communication skills than straight relationships."

We talk about our goals for the day, how much we'll record, which clients we'll reach out to for gigs, what kind of social media we'll work on, and then say our goodbyes.

I make my way to the booth and record another few hours of a woman in her forties starting over who has been gifted a cottage by the lake. She rebuilds the cottage, falls in love with a fisherman, and when her ex comes back to tell her he's always loved her, she tells him his kind of love wasn't good enough and she deserves better.

I cry at the end of the chapter, even though it's happy.

This.

This is what I want.

The cottage, the fisherman, and the absolute certainty I am worth loving well.

# 11. Signing

Somehow, by some miracle or mistake, I get a house. It's so much smaller than the one we've been living in, and somehow, it is so much homier. There is a beautiful kitchen with an island. The floors are black-and-white tile, the walls a robin's-egg blue. It looks like a fairy-tale cottage with its stone front and ivy climbing up to the roof. The colors in the dining and living rooms are lake colors: light gray with a hint of blue, the color of a stormy sky.  The living room is a deep blue like the color of the lake after a sandbar. There's a fireplace. There are three bedrooms and a bathroom that's been newly updated.

There is a backyard with a lush, wild garden and a huge deck. Maybe there will be parties here.

As soon as I walked in the door with the realtor, I said, "Let's make an offer, please. This is the one." And, somehow, they accepted.

The house had been on the market for a while, waiting for me I'd like to think, but when I look at the paperwork it says the house has been treated for termites.

I don't care. This is my house. This house is meant for me. Maybe it's a little broken, a little—oh, God—infested, but who cares. I can deal with broken. I understand it.

***

A few weeks later, I am sitting in the title office and I have signed all the paperwork selling my house and buying the new one. I don't breathe, even when my realtor hands me a bottle of Dom Perignon and the keys and says, "It's all yours."

I don't breathe or feel, or think to hope or dream or accept until I am sitting in the parking lot of the lease office, and then every feeling rushes over me in a wave.

I have been so afraid, so afraid of making the wrong choice, of not having a place to live, of not being safe. I have been on edge for years, trying not to say the wrong thing. Trying to be supportive and calm and loving. My body is a wire stretched taut, about to snap, and in the parking lot, it does. Because I am holding the keys to my future in the palm of my hand. It's not a metaphor. It's a literal, tangible thing. These keys will open the door to whatever my life is going to be.

Matthew took most of the big furniture in the split so there won't be much to move. My kids and I will move our few belongings left into the house, and eventually, I'll buy new things. A dining room table. Chairs. New plates. Rugs. Blankets. Things to make us feel soft and comfortable and warm.

There is a banister leading upstairs and I will wrap it with garland and twinkle lights at Christmas, and there will be an orange fire in the fireplace, crackling. We'll have meals together here. There will be times when the kids and I fight, and times when we hug. The dogs will find places to curl up and call their own. I can sit on my back deck and have Erin over and we can drink wine and watch the leaves tremble on the giant oak tree. Watch the world darken. Watch the night birds come out. "Night birds" that I know are bats, but the renaming of them makes them not so scary.

And sitting here in the parking lot, I remember all these things, while clenching the key now warm in my hand.

There are tears. Of course there are. And guilt. How did I get so lucky? I don't deserve this. How did this happen?

But it did happen. I made this happen. It isn't a gift from the universe. It's something I did. Something I chose.

When I get it together enough and wipe the makeup that's smeared from my eyes, I take a huge breath, feel myself enter my body, and I drive *home.*

# 12. The Doctor's Office

I'm not naked and wrapped in a paper sheet, but I might as well be with how vulnerable I feel. "I'm here because I'm exhausted. I'm really exhausted. And we've been treating all these issues separately, but what if they're part of a bigger whole? What if something else is going on?"

The doctor looks at me and I'm waiting for her to say I'm imagining things, but instead she says, "Tell me."

I take a deep breath. I'll need it to get all this out. "I take Trazadone to sleep. I've gained twenty pounds in the last three years. Last year, I had severe anemia and dizziness. I mean, I felt like I'd pass out when I walked to the mailbox, and the bleeding during my period was just awful. I couldn't leave the house. So then I had an ablation. That helped with the bleeding, of course, and eventually the anemia, but I'm still not right. I'm exhausted all the time. Not regular exhausted, but a tired-in-my bones exhaustion. I can't get through the day without a nap. And my hair is falling out. It really is. It's a noticeable thing. A real thing. I'm not imagining these symptoms. Look at my scalp! I'm forty-eight and I'm going bald. Or bald-ish. And maybe it's indulgent or vain or whatever but I just can't. I can't be forty-eight and single again, and be overweight and bald and completely unlovable. I just can't do it."

We just blink at each other.

"That's a lot," she says. Then she types some stuff down. "Any stress lately?"

I roll my eyes. Seriously? Where do I begin? I take another breath. This is the day for just saying it all, I guess. For finally coming clean.

"Besides the pandemic and lockdown, and every awful political and social meltdown happening in the world there's this, here's the laundry list: Surgery from the ablation, got divorced, sold a house, bought a house, moved into a house, apparently destroyed my ex's life, his family disowned me, I can't see my own family, a friend committed suicide due to the loneliness of lockdown. I'm terrified of getting Covid, if I lose my voice I can't work, and did I mention the hair falling out? I did? Am I stressed? Am I? I'm stressed in every molecule of my being. Every atom in my body hurts. My eyelashes hurt. My toes hurt. My heart, oh, my heart. You better believe that hurts too. That hurts the most. I hurt. I fucking hurt."

She stops typing and just looks at me, and I sort of want to hug her for looking at me. I'm so tired of being invisible that it is a relief, an utter relief, to have someone look at me. "I hear you," she says. "Here's what we can do. Let's get a full blood work on you. Let's see what's going on. And in the meantime, how about an antidepressant? Maybe not forever, maybe just for now? Just to get you through?"

"Just to get me through?"

She nods.

The idea that this is a space I can pass through, like passing from the state line of Michigan into Ohio is shocking. I don't have to stay here? I can just pass through this, eventually? That's possible?

"Yes," I say with all my heart. "Please. And, oh, thank you. Thank you so much."

# 13. Putting Things Together

Erin comes over wearing overalls and carrying a power drill with a bow on it. "It's for you. Don't say no. Can you drill things?"

"No," I say.

"I told you not to say that. The first thing we should do in America is give every woman a power drill and teach her how to use it. Screwing things is very satisfying."

I hold it in my hands. It's lighter than I expected. And I'm terrified.

"Why am I so scared?" I ask.

"Right? Isn't it dumb? It's a fucking tool and we're conditioned to need men to do everything. This is something I can teach you."

So she does.

She also puts together all of the furniture I ordered that came in huge boxes with diagrams and a million pieces, and so many steps I felt completely overwhelmed, like I was receiving directions on how to do something but in a different language. At first, I try to help her, but then we both agree I should sit back and eat pizza and post things to Instagram. It's a better use of my energy. "Plus," Erin says, "I fucking love this shit. And honestly, I don't want to share this with you."

So we pass the night. I eat too much pizza and she puts together a credenza and a love seat. Then she teaches me to drill.

"Where do you want this picture?" she asks.

"I don't know," I say. Because I don't. Matthew hung up all of our pictures and most of them were his. His art. His style. These are a few posters of up north we'd had framed and he let me keep them. "Here?" I ask.

"Don't ask me. Tell me," she says, and I'm pretty sure she's training me for something. Maybe life.

"Here," I say.

"Okay, so you take the screw and it's got this magnet and then you just put a little pressure and then..." zzzzzzzztt "Voila! Now you do it."

I'm shaking. My hand is shaking. Then I get mad because it's a fucking screw. It's a screw and a wall and a stupid photo. This is not the end of the world, this is hanging a fucking picture but it is also everything else. It is the audacity I had of wanting something more: more from my life, of demanding something better, and using this drill proves I am up to the challenge, I can handle this, I can learn and change and grow and...

*Zzzzzzzzztt*

"Holy shit!" I cry.

"Pretty awesome, right?"

I. Fucking. Love. It.

"I'm going to have to buy some more pictures," I say and then I grab another screw.

# 14. Holidays

The holidays are approaching and it is terrifying.

It shouldn't be, and maybe it's dramatic to say that it is, but there we are. I'm scared.

"Why are you so scared?" my life coach asks me. We're sitting in her office. Soft velvet couch, plump pillows, desert colors. It has a little flair of the 1970s in here, but the colors are less abrasive. There's less orange and brown, more rose and sand.

I'd stopped seeing my life coach because Matt asked me to. Now that there is no Matt, I can do what I want. And seeing her helps me. She asks me the questions that I'm afraid to give voice to.

'This is hard to put into words," I say. My throat is hot.

"Where do you feel it?" she asks.

"Feel what? The words?"

"The words. The pain. Where is it sitting right now?"

"In my throat. It's choking me a little."

She nods. "You know much about chakras?"

I shake my head. I'm not into the woo-woo.

"The throat chakra symbolizes expression and speaking the truth. And that's where your pain is sitting?"

This time I nod.

So.

Fuck.

Maybe I need to read into chakras.

I'm choking on my words because speaking the truth is hard. Just speaking is hard. We don't say the things we need to say, and this—beyond anything else in my life—is the thing I'm trying to change. I don't want to be silent. I want to say what I feel, feel what I feel. I want to live through it.

I try again. My voice has a strangled sound to it and each word feels like a plum being plucked from my throat. "I'm afraid of Christmas because when I open presents with the kids, there won't be anything for me."

She doesn't say anything for a time. She just looks at me. Breathes with me. I can see sympathy and compassion in her expression and it is soothing. But it also hurts. To be this vulnerable.

It's not that I need presents. It's not about that. It's something more and I can't quite get at it.

"Say more," she says.

I take a breath. "My husband would organize getting the kids to get something for me. Take them shopping. Pick something out for me. And he'd give me things too. Mostly joke gifts, but it was fun to laugh on Christmas morning. But this year...there isn't going to be anything for me. I don't have family that sends gifts. We're so broken we don't even speak to each other. And I could take my kids shopping, force them to get something for me, but that's not what I want."

"What do you want?"

The words float and shiver in front of me. Waiting.

"I want to matter enough to be remembered on Christmas morning. And I am not."

Suddenly, the final plum in my throat evaporates. I can breathe again. The tightness in my throat relaxes. This is what I'm afraid of.

I'm afraid I don't matter.

I'm afraid you pluck me off of the planet, and there wouldn't even be a vacant space to show I'd been there.

She nods.

We sit for a time. I start to breathe more normally and the heat in my throat stops burning. I know what the fear is. I've named it. Now I can deal with it.

"This Christmas is going to suck," she says. I laugh. A little. And she laughs a little. "It just is. It's going to fucking suck. And you know what? You're going to get through it. You're going to get through the morning and the day and the night. And then you're going to get through the next one and the next. So maybe there isn't a present for you this year. Not in a box anyway. The present for you this year...is you. You being there with your kids in a way that is authentic, true, and safe. And maybe next year, things will be different. Next year, things will for sure be better than this year."

These words, these simple words acknowledging the truth of how awful this is, make me somehow believe I can get through this.

I smile then. A real one. A face-stretched-wide-and-sparkling-eyes smile. Because this? I can deal with this. This Christmas is going to fucking suck, and I'll get through it.

I do matter.

I fucking do.

# 15. DATING

"I think I'm ready to start dating again. The divorce is final and..." I mean to keep going but Erin interrupts me. She knows what I'm going to say anyway.

"Fuck yeah. You don't have to justify anything, you know. If you want to date, date."

"I feel like I have to justify it. I feel like wanting to date is kind of, I don't know, a failure."

Erin looks at me. She just looks at me.

"I'm reading all the books and listening to all the podcasts, and I know I'm supposed to be enough. For myself. I'm supposed to be..." I pause. I'm really struggling with this concept. "I'm really struggling with this concept," I say.

She says, "I don't want to date anyone again ever, but I get it. That's me. It's different for you. You're in a different space." Erin and her husband are still together. They're working on things, but I wonder for how long. She continues, "You want companionship, yeah? Someone to share time with when your kids are with their dad. And you want sex. Good sex, hopefully."

I nod. She gets it. "Yeah. I do. I want that. And I want to watch movies with someone and go out to a restaurant. I want to get dressed up and be excited and I want that thing that happens when you haven't touched someone yet, but you're sitting next to each other and the hairs rise on your arms just being near them."

"Fuuuuccccck," Erin says. It's an agreement.

"But it feels weak."

"You're not weak for wanting someone in your life."

"But I had someone. I had Matt. And I didn't want him anymore."

"You didn't want Matt anymore because you became his mother. He didn't want you either. Not all of you. Not the full woman you. Things change. People change. Fuck, *wanting* changes. You didn't want Matt as a partner. You thought you didn't want a partner at all, and now you do. Go with it."

I'm getting emotional again. Everything lately is so right at the surface that if you just touch my skin, my bones and sinew are suddenly exposed. "Erin?" I ask. "What if no one wants me back?"

What she should say, what I expect her to say is, "Of course someone will want you! You are wantable! It's fine!" If she said that,

I'd try to believe her, but I really wouldn't. Instead though, she surprises me. She lets my question dangle between us and she thinks about it. She really thinks about it.

"I can see why that would be terrifying," she says. "Welp. You're not going to know until you try."

That night I put up a profile on one of the apps. I don't know what to say, what pictures to post. How do I come across as stable, sexy, and desirable? I imagine all the profiles of all the other women and how men my age will probably go for thirty-year-olds. I am not enough. I can't compete with long hair and makeup and yoga bodies. I don't know how to date after ten years. It's a different world and I'm a different person. And what do I want, anyway? Do I want a relationship? I think I do. Then I think of how wrong things went with Matt and how, in the end, I hated him and I don't know if I can go through that again. I don't know how I can.

I publish the profile.

I'm terrified.

What if no one wants me?

Worse, what if someone does?

***

I meet Havel a few weeks later. I'm not sure he's real. He can't be real. His pictures are adorable. He's fit. He's only a few years older than me. What does he see in me that made him reach out and suggest we meet for a walk? We don't seem to have a ton in common, but there's not a lot on his profile to go on anyway. He seems like that kind of man I've always wanted to date. But what does he see in me?

Then I try to check in with myself and give my self-loathing a rest for a bit. Just for tonight. I'm just meeting him for a walk. It's practice. It's not a big deal. Stop questioning and just enjoy. Try to enjoy, anyway.

We meet at 6 p.m. and it is still winter enough to be pitch dark. The temperature is right on the edge of freezing and snow falls in big, fat flakes. We decide to meet in Gaslight Village. I know the area well. It's well lit. There are popular restaurants in the downtown area. We will meet outside the library and take a walk. I'm not exactly sure it's him when I pull up and park. He doesn't see me so I double-check the profile and the pictures.

He's shorter than I thought. And much more handsome. He has the physique of a runner, lean and lithe. Such a contrast to Matt. He's wearing a puffy blue jacket and when I walk up to say hi, his blue eyes are the color of clear ice. He's stunning.

I'm afraid I've disappointed him, just by being me.

"Hi," I say.

He smiles. It seems genuine. "Hello! Shall we walk?"

"You still want to?" I'm nervous. It shows.

"That is why we are here, yes? To walk. To get to know each other."

There's something in his voice. A slight accent. I nod. And we start to walk. Of course, things are still shut down because of the pandemic, so what should be a bustling area is eerily quiet. It didn't even occur to me! I can hear the snow fall and the faint sizzle of the gaslit lanterns.

I slip once on the ice and he steadies me with his hand on the small of my back for just a moment. He doesn't think about it. It's just a reflex.

We walk by the closed restaurants. No Chinese takeout. No gastro pub. No South Carolina shrimp and grits. Just takeout. Havel and I don't wear masks and I'm a little grateful. It's nice to see his face. I hope he likes seeing mine.

We chat. He's from Czechoslovakia. He left in 1991 after the uprising. He doesn't give details, but I can fill in the blanks. There's a lot of sadness there, probably more than I can imagine. He says life is much better here and he is grateful. He was married for twenty years and now he is not. They came over here together. "So much darkness," he says.

I don't think he's talking about the light leaving around us.

We talk about cooking. He likes to make bread. I tease him that I make a mean lentil dish thinking no one likes lentils and he seems to light up at the idea. "You make the mean lentil dish and I will make the bread."

He asks me to tell him about my job of narrating audiobooks. "It's fun," I say. "It's a great fit for me."

"You have a nice voice," he says.

"This is my speaking voice. I change it slightly when I narrate."

"How?" he asks.

I drop my register a bit, add in a little velvet to my voice. It sounds sexy when I say, "I don't know. I just lower it a little."

He stops walking and I take a few steps before I realize. Then I stop and turn around. He looks at me. His blue eyes spark.

"You have a *very* nice voice," he says. There is something in the way he says that. I feel the hairs on my arm raise.

"You do too."

We talk about our jobs, our kids, things we like to do. It is easier than I thought it would be, but it is still not comfortable. I feel a little wrong, like Matt will be disappointed in me. But there is no more Matt and me. There is just me and it is okay that I am doing this.

Eventually, we walk back to our cars. The snow is now transitioning to freezing rain. Our coats are wet. We stand in front of the library and I am trying to remember how to say goodbye to a stranger.

"Let us get some wine," he says.

I laugh. Not the goodbye I was expecting. "Oh, that's a nice offer. But where? How?" I motion to all the dead restaurants. You can't just go and get a drink anymore. You can't just get to know someone slowly in the gold warmth of a restaurant. You aren't even supposed to show your face to someone anymore, let alone stand outside talking in the icy rain.

"There is a grocery store. We buy some wine and some dark chocolate and we see where the night goes."

"Oh," I say. And then my mind says Ohhhhhhh. He wants to come home with me. Or he wants me to go to his house. This attractive man, this accented, fit man, wants to sleep with me. Well, not sleep. He doesn't want to sleep. This man wants to fuck me. Me. Of the too puffy face and wide hips. The soft belly. Maybe it's because the lighting is too dark. Maybe he's mistaken. Maybe he doesn't know what he wants.

No.

That's not true. This is a man who knows what he wants. He wants me.

For a moment I think of sipping wine with him, of tasting dark chocolate. Of being inside a warm house. Would we talk more or would he just kiss me? What would his lips feel like, the scruff of his jaw dragging across my hungry skin?

But I can't.

I can't.

You don't go home with someone you met online. You don't have sex with a stranger. You don't have sex with anyone right now because of Covid. I shouldn't even be dating. This is ridiculous. What am I doing out in the dark in the ice with this man who looks at me while his eyes spark?

"I'm sorry," I say. "I can't."

He holds his hands up and shrugs his shoulders as if to say, "This is the way of the world. Life is disappointment."

I shake his hand. I tell him good night. I go home alone and regret all the things I don't allow myself to do, like live.

# 16. YES

There is a common scene in romcom movies and books where the heroine closes the door, leans against it, and sends a puff of air to get the bangs out of her eyes. Her heart is clearly palpitating.

Well, *something's* clearly palpitating.

When I get home, do I lean against the door, breathing heavily, palpitating...everywhere? I might as well be.

I could have a stranger in my home right now. A strange, Czechoslovakian could be in my home right now, his work-rough hands under my sweater, reaching for the clasp of my bra.

But that's not what's happening. I am in my home, by myself, smart and safe and secure and...and...

A small voice is in my mind.

ME:
Why do you always have to be so good?
ALSO ME:
What do you mean? I'm not being good. I'm being responsible. It's not safe to invite someone you don't know into your home. Especially inviting someone into your home during a pandemic.
ME: If the pandemic has taught us anything, it's that there's so much living to do.
ALSO ME:
I am living.
ME:
You're fucking running. You run from everything. You swaddle yourself in rules and have-tos and shoulds and should nots. It's all just a lame attempt at control. And you can control things, I guess. You can control your risk. You can control the amount of fun you have.
ALSO ME:
I am not the kind of person who has fun. I have relationships. I get married.
ME:
How's that working out for you?
ALSO ME:
Goddammit.

I tear my coat off. I'll just have some wine by myself and watch a movie. Maybe I'll masturbate. Nothing sad in that. A woman should know how to please herself.

ME:
You have been pleasing yourself for years.
Can't someone else do it for a while?

I'm about to tell myself to fuck off, when something curious happens. A text. I pull my phone out of my pocket and it's Havel. He doesn't say *so nice to meet you.* He doesn't say *I would like to see you again.* He doesn't say *I had a lovely time.* No. He says

HAVEL:
I am only a yes away.

What would I do right now if I had the freedom to act on my desires? If I silenced all the inner rules? What would I say?

I take a deep breath.

I text YES.

# 17. Whirlwind

He comes to my door carrying a bottle of red wine and a Lindt bar of dark chocolate with orange. He is smiling. There are crinkles around his eyes. His cheeks are pink from the cold.

"Can I come in?" he asks.

Never invite a vampire into your home, my brain says.

"Yes," I say.

I take the wine and the chocolate from him, confused as to what I'm supposed to do now. Pour him a glass? Cut the chocolate into pieces and put it on a serving platter? What should I serve with it? Make a quick charcuterie board, maybe. Maybe this is what I do. I have men over and offer them a charcuterie board and my vagina. Maybe I put the charcuterie board over my vagina and...

"Hey," he says.

I refocus.

He unzips his coat and I tell him to hang it by the door. I set the wine and the chocolate in my kitchen. I can feel him behind me. It's not scary. No. That's not what I'm feeling. What I'm feeling is something else entirely.

"Do you?" My question doesn't even make sense. I start and turn around. He's taken off his hat. He has less hair than I expected, but that smile is lighting up his whole body.

"Come here," he says and reaches for me.

The kiss is warm and soft, teasing and eager. His hands touch my face and I feel such an ache in me, as if I have been so thirsty and he is finally giving me a drink.

My body warms. More than warms; it melts.

Oh, to be kissed! To have my face touched. To watch his hands tremble a bit with the buttons of my shirt, slowly undoing them one by one. To stand in my bright kitchen with my shirt at my feet, in my jeans and my black lacy bra while he kisses his way down my neck and then touches the line where my breasts meet. He kisses there too and then I can't stand it anymore. I can't stand the slow gentle kisses, the tongue on my bare breast. I want more. I am filled with wanting.

I *am* wanting.

I don't know who does what but my jeans are unzipped, and I step out of them, briefly grateful I wore cute matching underwear. He doesn't even look at the bra and panties set, he's already pulling them off me, his hand reaching for my mound and then his fingers quickly find their way inside me. He nibbles at my neck and I gasp because it feels so good.

Then his sweater and shirt and pants are off and he is naked in my kitchen. Between the kisses I laugh a little. "You don't wear underwear?" I ask.

"Why bother with this? It is not necessary. This is all that is necessary." He kisses my throat and then he presses our bare bodies against each other. I feel his hand reach for me and then two of his fingers are inside me, his tongue exploring my breasts, my neck, my mouth, my cheeks, my eyelids, and my clavicle.

I'm not thinking of anything right now. Not relationships or marriage or soul connections. Not regrets and mistakes and embarrassing failures.

The only thing I am thinking is how fit and beautiful this man is, how is chest is firm and speckled with hair. How his cock in my hand keeps growing and how I never really thought a penis could be beautiful, but evidently, I was wrong.

All I can think is that I Want. I want him. I want him now. In my kitchen, in the living room, in my bed.

"Come," he says. I laugh a little because I'm so turned on I could orgasm with one more breath, but he means for me to follow him.

He doesn't know where to go so I laugh and smile. I can feel the smile reach my eyes, my heart, and my toes.

I lead him to my bed.

It is frenzied and passionate and so satiating.

This is what it is to be wanted. This is what it is to want and to receive.

This is what it is to have a need met, and all I had to do was say, "Yes."

# 18. The Loop

"So how are Matthew and the kids?" my mom immediately asks. Not even hello first.

I shouldn't have answered the phone. My ability to deal with this is in the negative zone. "Mom, Matthew and I aren't together. We broke up last year. The divorce has been final for a couple of months."

"What? Why didn't you tell me?"

I can hear the frustration in her voice. The hurt. It's two in the afternoon and I can picture my mom in her apartment: she's a hoarder. She's crammed in there, towers of stuff around her. Last time I was there, two years ago, she no longer had a place left to sleep on the bed. It was piled high with boxes bursting at the seams. I don't know how she manages, how she bathes or eats or sleeps, but I also can't fix her. I've tried so many times to fix her, to save her, and it just isn't possible. And now this. Now, her mind is slipping. Looping. Dementia, maybe, but probably Alzheimer's. Her great aunt had Alzheimer's. Everyone hated her great aunt.

"I did tell you. It was a long process." I keep my voice calm and even, although my whole body is triggered right now.

"What happened?"

"We grew apart. He was depressed a lot and I..."

"Oh, I get that. I'm depressed a lot. It's really hard. I only have thirty dollars in my bank account. I accidentally overspent by three hundred! I don't even know how I did that or what I bought. And my rent is due and I'm just not sure what I should do."

The need from her reaches across the miles, through the air, and burrows into my veins. She can't remember my husband and I divorced or that I am trying to start over or I am struggling. She doesn't understand how tight money is and how afraid I am of the future and not being able to support myself and the kids. She can't recognize what I need most right now is a mom, and she can't be that for me. She needs me to parent her, and there's nothing left in me to give.

She can, however, remember to call me when she needs money.

This time I don't offer.

"I'm doing great!" she says, her voice bright and tight. I don't know if she's actively lying or if she believes she is doing great. "I'm so happy with Frank. He's so wonderful. Did I tell you that he is a huge Star Trek fan and that—"

I interrupt because I can't hear this story again. "Twenty years ago, he went to a convention and got his picture with Shatner. Yes. You told me."

I'm being cruel. It feels cruel. She doesn't like it when I interrupt a story of hers. It throws her.

I want to throw her.

"Oh. Well. I am so happy. You don't have to worry about me. I'm doing great. Except I only have thirty dollars in my bank account. I accidentally overspent by three hundred dollars! I don't even know how I did that or what I bought. And my rent is due and I'm just not sure what I should do."

I tell her I'll call my brother. He's in charge of her money. I'll transfer some to him to cover the rent. If I give her cash, she'll just spend it on more stuff to fill her apartment. Magazines, newspapers, things she finds in bulk on sale. It's all just stuff to tether her to the earth, maybe, as her brain tries to float away.

"Oh, that would be wonderful! Okay. I have to go. Frank and I are at the grocery store. Did you know he was a Star Trek fan?"

"No, I didn't," I say. I'm not crying, because there aren't any tears left, but I can feel the need for tears stuck in my throat.

"Give my love to the kids and Matthew. He's such a wonderful man. I'm so glad you have him in your life."

"Me too," I say. I hang up.

She never asked how I am, but then again, what would it matter? She wouldn't remember.

# 19. Gifts

I've just told Erin about the awkward Christmas gift exchange Matt and I had last night. "I got you something," he'd said. "Can I drop it off?" I'd said yes. He'd come over and we exchanged gifts, and it was terrible and awkward, and also nice to talk to him. Weirdly comforting. I'm telling Erin all of this. "I mean, what are you supposed to get the person you've been married to for ten years, but now you're divorced and you don't even know what his schedule is tomorrow? Should I get him something? Should I ignore getting him a Christmas present? Where's the manual for what you do in this situation?"

Erin grabs a slice of bread and dips it in the spicy olive oil. They don't offer bread service at this restaurant, but Erin somehow always manages to get them to bring us some. "Fucking gluten free culture," she says. "Every restaurant should have bread service."

I agree.

"So? What did you do? Did you get him something?"

"I did. I got him chowder."

Erin snort-laughs and I can't help but laugh too. Married for ten years, all the shit we went through, all the sex we had in the beginning, all the Christmases and birthdays and holidays, and it all ends with a three-pack gift of frozen seafood chowder.

"He likes chowder," I say.

"You don't have to justify it to me. Chowder sounds like the perfect gift. Here's the end of our marriage. And here's your chowder."

I take a piece of bread and dip it in the oil. God, it's so good. I don't understand why it's not on the menu. I'd come here and just eat bread with olive oil and swallow it down with red wine. We've ordered a full meal but I have a feeling we'll both be taking home leftovers.

I think of Matthew sitting across from me in my dream kitchen, the kitchen I never had with him, but have given myself. I brewed us coffee. Grabbed the milk from the fridge and handed him the sugar bowl. I know how he likes his coffee and I could've fixed it for him, but it somehow felt too intimate. It's not my job anymore to fix his coffee, so he did it himself, and I'm not sure, but maybe it made both of us sad.

"It was kind of an awful moment," I say to Erin.

"Oh no! Why? He didn't get you anything?"

"No, he did. He got me a gift basket."

Erin snorts again, but I'm not laughing. It's actually heartbreaking. I say, "No, you don't understand. You know how I love gift baskets. They're like my favorite thing on the planet. I don't know why. I just find them incredibly exciting. All these goodies wrapped in cellophane presented to you in a bounty. And he put this gift basket together himself. Told them what to put in it and everything."

"And? I'm confused. This is bad?"

"He got me gourmet cheese, this kind I had once and loved. He looked for my favorite kind of wine, something red, something full bodied, something with legs. He printed out the label from the store that said 'Hints of cinnamon and cherry. This wine has great legs.' There was–fuck–dark chocolate and fig jam. Gourmet crackers. A wine stop made out of a Petoskey stone. Mushroom jerky. All of it in a beautiful basket."

Erin isn't eating. She's just listening.

"These are all the things I love. These are the little details no one knows I love, but he knows it. Yet all the time we were married, he never once got me a gift basket. They were always joke gifts. A letter from Bigfoot. A bobblehead that looks like me. They were gifts to make you laugh, but not make you connect, you know? And this gift? This gift is everything I ever wanted wrapped up in plastic and with a shiny bow."

"That fucker," she says. "All this time he knew you and he could've..."

"All this time he knew me and he could've loved me. But he chose not to. And now he gives me this thoughtful gift and I don't really understand it, except that it's incredibly kind and incredibly mean at the same time."

"To be fair," Erin says, "He probably feels the same way about the chowder."

I nod.

"Are you going to throw it out?"

"The gift basket? Fuck no! I love that shit. I thought, maybe, what do you think, I could have a party instead?"

# 20. POETRY

ME: I wrote a tiny poem today.
HAVEL: Did you? You write poetry?
ME: Apparently, I do now. I wrote it for you.
HAVEL: What is it?

I take a deep breath and send the picture. I typed the poem on a typewriter and snapped a photo of it. Something about seeing the old font typed on a piece of paper is appealing to me. The ink smudged and there was a typo I corrected with pen. It is messy, but also there is something alive about it.

ME:
Even hours later
I can still feel your
heated kiss
against
my hungry skin
HAVEL: ...
HAVEL: ...
HAVEL: I like this. Write me another one.

It is morning and I am still in my pajamas, braless, no makeup, hair mussed. I'm drinking my coffee black because I've been fasting. I should not feel sexy right now, but the idea of writing a poem to Havel right now is so exciting that my body starts to alight.

I think for a moment, head to the typewriter, hit the keys. Take a picture and send it to him.

ME: I want to explore
the landscape of you
with my lips.
This time, his answer is immediate.
HAVEL: I can be at your house in half an hour.
I smile.
ME: Yes.

# 21. Doing the Work

"I'm really confused," I say. My life coach and I are meeting on Zoom since Covid is spiking again. It isn't safe to talk to someone face-to-face anymore, or to share the same air. I'm sitting in my kitchen and her face floats before me, my computer balanced on a stack of books so the angle is flattering to my neck. Every once in a while, I step back and realize how sci-fi modern living has become.

She's in her office and I can almost smell the essential oil. It's comforting. "Confused about what?"

"Yes," I say.

She laughs. "So...all of it? Confused about all of it?"

I take a deep breath.

I'm going to need the oxygen.

I say, "Yes. I'm confused about all of it. My life. What do I do now that I'm here? Where do I go? I'm confused about dealing with my mom. I put firm boundaries between us and now...it's like I have to break those boundaries. She was never a parent to me and now she needs me to parent her, and I don't want to. I'm confused about dating. About wanting to date. About how the fuck do you get to know someone new when you're starting from zero with them? It used to be I'd meet someone at college and take classes with them or have study times, or meet at a bar with our friends. But I haven't been in college in two decades. Or when I was in theater, I'd meet someone in a show. They weren't all gay. Or maybe they were, but they still were interested in my breasts. I met Matthew in theater. We had the same circles. We just knew each other. But now? I meet someone on an app and then what? What questions do I ask? How do you form a connection when there is nothing to start from except a few pictures or a couple of texts where you awkwardly ask how you're each doing? *How are you? I'm doing good. How are you?* I'm confused about Havel. We have this intense physical connection and it's amazing. I had an orgasm last night that I think I'm still feeling. Sorry if that makes you feel awkward."

"I'm good," she says.

"And when we're not having sex there's just all this silence. Like, this massive silence. It's terrible. I tried to have a conversation with him last night, and I just didn't know what to say. *What are your interests? How was work? What did you do today?* I could ask those questions, try to establish, I don't know, something, but the truth is, I didn't really care. But I don't particularly like just having sex. I mean, I like sex, and I really like sex with Havel but I want something more."

"Okay," she says. "So your mom. Boundaries. Dating. Intimacy. Havel. Anything else?"

"I'm also really confused about what to make the kids for dinner tonight. My son is upping his protein to gain weight and my daughter is going vegetarian, so I know fuck all what to do. I really don't want to make three meals."

"So don't."

"What?" I honestly don't think I heard her correctly.

"Don't make three meals. Make one. Make the one you want. If they don't like it, they can make a sandwich."

My jaw drops.

This has literally never occurred to me, the idea that at fifteen and sixteen my children are capable of making a sandwich. The relief of this possibility is so intense that I start to cry. I don't have to make three meals!!! They can make a fucking sandwich!!

It seems ridiculous, this realization, but it's not. It's big for me. After growing up in a dysfunctional home, I promised myself my kids would have routine and be cared for. They'd have good food that was freshly made. But maybe it's time to start letting them do some things. They weren't raised in a dysfunctional home, and they need to know how to make a sandwich.

"Make sure you're breathing," she says. She can tell I need the reminder.

I breathe for a bit. Let the tears work their way through my system. Letting go, changing, is hard work, and my mind is spinning.

My life coach will ask me questions if I need her to, but mostly I think I just need to talk.

So I do. I tell her I don't want to tackle my issue with my mom right now, I'm not strong enough, but I do want to talk about last night. "Last night, I wore this gold-colored Henley and a pair of jeans. It's new for me, to wear clothes that are fitted, are revealing. It's a V-neck shirt and my boobs looked pretty great in it, and I felt good and sexy. I don't usually wear gold, but I decided what the hell.

I'm trying to dress like the person I want to be, instead of the person I've been."

"And?"

"And Havel comes over and starts kissing me. Immediately comes in the door and we're kissing and he pushes me up against the wall. To be honest, I kind of guided him to do that. And then for a minute, he froze. He just stopped. There was a beam of light streaming in from the window and into my eyes, and he brushed the hair away from my eyes and said, 'The sunlight on you in this gold shirt and the blue of your eyes, it is just so beautiful.' Then the sex and the orgasm."

"And you're confused about that?"

"I can't explain it, but it felt like a goodbye. We usually text during the day. There's been nothing. I think last night was the last time. It was goodbye sex. He said I was beautiful and I don't think I'm going to see him again. I don't know what I did wrong."

"Did you do anything wrong? Didn't you approach this with the intention of being exactly who you are?"

"I did, and I have been, and that's the thing. That's the really hard thing. I have been exactly who I am, and we have nothing to talk about and no connection. What if there's something wrong with me? What if I'm not enough?"

She thinks about that.

"Does that feel true?" she asks. "That you're not enough?"

"Yes?"

Even over Zoom, I can get what her expression is telling me.

I say, "I don't know. Honestly. Can you help me here because I can't see or understand or process. I feel like I'm standing in the middle of a cornfield and all I see is corn. And I don't even like corn."

"Not all relationships last forever. You've had a fun time with him. Maybe that's the lesson here. Maybe you needed to know you can be desirable and have a fulfilling sexual relationship that isn't a marriage. And maybe, the real truth is, he isn't enough for you."

I think about that.

Is that possible?

"He's not enough?"

"You tell me," she says.

I think about it. I put my hand to my heart and take a deep breath, checking in with myself. And then I nod. "He isn't enough for me," I say. "I want someone I can talk to. Someone I can have a conversation with. I want to have great sex, but I also want a deep connection. I want to do things with someone. Go out. Go hiking. Go to a cottage, a movie, a restaurant. I want more."

"You want more," she says. "And now you know."

I smile. "Now I know."

# 22. NEEDS

I'm talking to my aunt on the phone. She's been a second mom to me over the years since my mom wasn't ever really available emotionally or physically, and now not *mentally* available either. My aunt is also a therapist so she's excellent to talk to, and good at making boundaries.

I wish she wasn't so good at boundaries.

As a kid, I dreamed of her and my uncle taking me and my brother in so we could have the same kind of life my cousins did: parents who lived in a fancy brick Colonial house in East Lansing by Michigan State University, rules that we couldn't drink pop or we'd get night terrors, things we had to do to earn an allowance. We'd have a normal life, instead of the freedom and chaos we had with my mom. I was hungry for rules and structure. I ached for someone to care enough about me to say no.

When I talk to my aunt, I am grateful to talk to her, and sad I couldn't have been hers.

"It's been so long since we talked, honey. I'm really sorry about that."

"It's okay," I say. My uncle has COPD and with Covid running rampant, they are on strict lockdown from the outside world. I haven't seen them in two years. "You don't owe me anything."

"Well, it's nice talking to you."

"It is nice talking to you too." My throat hurts and I remind myself of the chakra and communication and pain and longing. These are feelings. I can get through it. I can talk through it. I have missed my aunt fiercely. "Tell me what's happening," I say.

"Whew. That's a big question. You'd think with us not leaving the house, nothing would be happening, but that's not the case. I made it through chemo. If you're going to have breast cancer, I guess I had the best kind. Caught it early, it's small, hasn't spread. Doctor appointments have been difficult to navigate. They shut so many procedures down. And your uncle isn't able to get the physical therapy he used to have for his lungs. They gave him videos to watch, but it's just not the same thing.

"I'd like to see your cousin. She had their baby and he's almost one and I've barely seen him. They're on lockdown too. I get my walks in with my friends. We're outside and masked up, but it's hard sometimes, you know? And it's challenging because with the lumpectomy. I can't really lift my arms high above my head and so it's hard to put things away like dishes and stuff. Your uncle can't really do it because he's on oxygen all the time and sometimes I just get a little mad, you know? Like it's so unfair that I can't put the pasta pot where it belongs. It just has to sit on my counter now."

This is the angriest I've ever heard her. It's not really angry at all, but coming from my aunt who is calm and steady, to hear her complain about anything is so rare that it's a little shocking. I think about that pasta pot sitting on her counter where it doesn't belong. We all have pasta pots right now.

It's a revelation, really.

I've been sitting in my own misery of the divorce, starting over, dating, and loneliness so I forgot that others are struggling too. Everyone is struggling, it seems. Just change the details, but we're all treading water, trying to keep our heads above the water. It's cliché, but it's true. We're all just trying to stay afloat.

My aunt's voice shifts a little with her next line. It softens. Loosens. "And I know you don't want to, honey, but we need to talk about your mom. We got a call from her apartment complex. They had a fire marshal check her apartment and, apparently, it's really bad. If she doesn't clean it out, they're going to evict her. It's a fire hazard. And we can't have your mom homeless. We can't. We have to do something."

When she says "We" what she means is me. I have to do something. I think of Mom and her hoarding. In her last apartment, my brother found a cardboard box that said Bill on it. "What's this, Mom?" he asked.

"Oh! That's Bill," she said.

My brother and I looked at each other. "Bill?"

"He was married to my friend Alma and they got in a huge fight. Turns out he was sleeping with a stripper. Can you believe that? At his age? Alma left him and moved to Florida. Then Bill died and Alma refused to pick him up. His ashes have been sitting at the fire department for two years, and I told them I'd take him. I went to send Bill to her, but apparently you can't send human remains in the mail, so he just hangs out in the closet right now."

This is my mother: tragic and deeply funny at the same time.

I shiver to think of what she has in her closets now. What is in the towers of stuff that she's filled her space with?

And I suddenly can't breathe. I can't focus on my aunt or having a conversation with her.

I'm overwhelmed.

Entirely overwhelmed.

It's physical, this reaction. It's my whole body, hijacked.

If my mom needs to move her stuff, it means I need to do it. She lives in a retirement community and I can't be exposed to Covid. If I get sick and lose my voice, I can't work. I can't get paid. I only have a few thousand dollars in the bank and if anything happens to me, that's it. Then my brain moves even more rapidly: *Hire movers. Get her a storage unit. You can organize everything from afar. You don't have to be there or deal with it directly.*

But who will pay for it?

You can't ask your aunt and uncle. It's not their job. And your brother lost his job due to all the restaurants shutting down, and he lives out of state and can't come home. So you have to do this. You have to use the last of your savings to rescue a mother, who is not really a mother to you at all, because if you don't, she will be homeless and you will have to let her into your home.

So I tell my aunt the truth. "I can't," I say, and the words are sharp in my throat. My throat bleeds with speaking. "I can't talk about this or process this right now. I need some time. I just...There's so much on my plate and I'm all alone. I'm here in this house and there is no one to help me. And I just don't have anything left. I don't have any energy to give more. I've given everything. I just got out of a marriage where I had to care for my husband, had to do everything, and now I'm still doing everything, only it's worse some days. And the money. God, the money is so stressful. And I just can't. I can't take on my mom right now. I shouldn't have to. I can't rescue her. I don't want to. I don't. I can't."

My aunt and I are silent. We just sit in it together, miles apart in our isolated homes, alone, and together. "I know you can't," she says. "We can help some. We can figure this out."

What I feel then is rage. Rage at my mother who in her illness and with her bad decisions continues to take and take and take. My aunt can't help my uncle and recover from cancer, and I can't heal and get strong from a lifetime of feeling neglected. We don't get the luxury of taking care of ourselves, because we have to take care of her.

"I'll come up with a plan," I say.

"Are you okay?" she asks.

"No," I say. "Are you?"

"No."

Then we laugh.

What else can we do?

# 23. Dates

I decide that dating is a numbers game. Eventually, pick enough numbers and you'll find the winning combination. Or whatever. I'm trying to make a lottery analogy, but it just isn't working. Date enough frogs, you eventually get a prince?

A prince sounds like a lot of work though. I'd rather have a nice man in a flannel shirt and jeans.

So, I start dating. I'm not exactly sure what I'm looking for: companionship, someone who's interested in me physically and emotionally, someone fun.

**DATE NUMBER ONE**

We meet at a little donut shop/coffeehouse about half an hour from my home. He texts me and says he's going to be late, so I sit at the table where my name is on a placard. It's weird and a little out of place. This does not seem like a place that has placards. There's a key to use the bathroom, and everything is in to-go cups, even the donuts.

I'm about to leave after twenty minutes of waiting, when the door swings open and he barrels in. He's a big man, and has a bit of a limp. I'm a little disappointed because we'd chatted a lot about my love of hiking and long walks, and I'm wondering now if he could keep up with me.

He smiles, and it's warm. I smile back. He's older than anyone I've dated. He turns sixty next month, but that's okay. I'm open to anything.

He says, "Oh, there you are. You look just like your pictures. Prettier than in your pictures. Your eyes are so blue, they're like, to my heart." He reaches for my hands and squeezes them. It's a little intense. And I am more than a little nervous.

"Uhm..."

"Do you like the flower and your name on the table? I asked them to do that. Gave them a little extra to make a card and put it on the table. They don't usually do that here."

"No. I wouldn't guess so. I mean, it's a donut shop."

He moves the open seat so it is right next to mine and he sits down. I lean back a little. I'm not sure I want him in my space.

"I like seeing your name with mine," he says. "We look good together, don't you think? I can just see it now at our wedding, our card on the front table, your name plus mine. More flowers though. We can do whatever you want."

"You're not serious, are you?" I think he's very serious. He studies my face for a moment, and I am sure what he sees there is pure panic. I wanted to start dating again. I don't ever want to be married.

"Serious? No. Of course not." He laughs a little, but not a real laugh. Then he's back to being intense. "But I can see it, can't you? Can I hold your hand?"

"Maybe later."

"When we're done with lunch, I'd like to take a walk with you and then maybe kiss you by your car."

"I don't think..."

"It's okay. I can be patient."

I don't know what to say to that, so I just say nothing. Then we sit in the silence. It's awkward. I say, "So. Uhm. Again, nice to meet you. So you said you have kids, yeah?"

"I do. Six of them. Most of them are adults."

"Six? Wow!"

"I'm a good Catholic. One of them is texting me now."

"Do you need to get that?"

"No it's just...it's just Sam. He's warning me not to be impulsive. Do I strike you as impulsive?"

"Ask me on our wedding night." Pause. "That was a joke."

**DATE NUMBER TWO**

ME: Erin, what do I do? I mean I'm sitting in this restaurant on Friday night
and he's ten minutes late. I already sent him a text to see if he's stuck in traffic, but he hasn't answered me.
ERIN: Did he confirm he was coming?
ME: Yes. Yesterday. But I haven't heard from him today. I'm so embarrassed.
What if he doesn't show up?
ERIN: Deep breaths, He'll show up. Of course he will.
ME: We only have this table for an hour and a half because of Covid restrictions.
ERIN: He's only ten minutes late.
ME: ....
ERIN: He's only fifteen minutes late.
ME: ....
ERIN: Did you order a cocktail?
ME: ....
ERIN: Fucking order a big martini and a burger. You deserve it. You look great and you have that table for another thirty minutes. Own that table. You've got this.
ERIN: Also, men are dicks. I'm so, so, so sorry.

**DATE NUMBER THREE**

I decide to meet this man because we both have writing in common. He's about ten years younger than me, which is weird to me, but don't men date younger women all the time? Why shouldn't a woman date a younger man? Plus, he asked me out, so why not? Maybe we'll have a ton to talk about with writing and words and thoughts and ideas.

He looks younger than his profile picture. Significantly younger. I'm worried his voice is going to crack. "Hello," he says and we shake hands. I feel like I'm meeting one of my son's friends. "You want to walk down and do some window-shopping? I haven't seen the new businesses here. I want to check the juice place. See what their prices are."

"Okay. Don't you live in town? You haven't been to the juice place yet?"

"No. I don't get out much. Have you ever been to the Bowdin Steakhouse?"

"No, I haven't tried it yet. Have you?"

"I looked at the prices. It's really expensive."

"Ah." We walk toward the juice place. I put a little more distance between us while we walk, just so we don't bump hands or something. "So you said earlier that you just moved back into town?"

"Well, it's a little embarrassing really. I moved back into town to get back on my feet. You know, I'm an artist, really, and I don't pay much attention to money and earning a lot of it you know, so I moved back to just get on my feet and..."

"Yeah. You said that. When did you move back?"

"In 2013."

"So eight years ago?"

"Yeah."

"To get back on your feet?"

"Yeah."

"So what you're telling me here is that you live with your parents."

"Yeah. You wanna get a hot chocolate? My treat."

**DATE NUMBER FOUR**

This one is only five years older than me. That's nice. We're meeting at my favorite restaurant in town, Rose's. It's right on the lake. I'd like to get a cocktail, maybe some food, but he'd mentioned coffee, so we order coffee instead. He's been talking for a while now. He is attractive. He has a nice voice. He has blue eyes. He is nice. Maybe this is someone with potential.

"My wife was a narcissist," he says. "I'm learning so much now. I'm in therapy. Are you?"

"Yep. I think we should all be in therapy. We should carry around therapists in our pockets."

"Could be useful. Did you have a moment when you knew?"

"Knew what?"

"Knew you were done? Did something happen to you and you just knew that was the final moment?"

I nod. Of course there was a moment. The moment is now part of my story. It's hard now to know how true it is because I've told it so many times, but I know it's true. The feelings are true. I try to explain it to him. "Yes. There was. I had a moment when...you know how Velcro is? How strong it is when it sticks together but when you pull it apart, it takes a lot of force, and then all of the sudden, you can feel it give way? It makes this horrible ripping noise and you can feel each side give up on the other?"

"I know that, yeah."

"We'd just had sex. My husband couldn't finish. He looked at me, and I'm still naked and he's naked, and he said he wasn't attracted to me. That was the moment. There was nothing left of our marriage after that." It is really painful to say this out loud, and I'm not sure why I did. I'm afraid he's not going to have anything to say to that. I mean, what do you say? Sorry your husband no longer wanted to fuck you? It sounds coarse. It sounds flippant. The truth is, my husband no longer wanted me on any level, and I responded to him with rage. But the man nods and starts talking again.

"I had a similar thing. We weren't naked, but it felt that way. She was yelling at me. Just yelling at me, pointing her finger right in my face, and I just let it wash right over me, yeah, yeah, whatever, you hate me, okay, I'm terrible. She was gaslighting me. I didn't know what that was then, but I do now. Brainwashing me to think I was less than. I didn't hear most of it right up until the end and then she screamed at me 'You are incapable of love! You are unlovable!' That broke me. Right in two. Velcro ripped apart."

"But that wasn't a true statement," I say. It was a terrible thing to say. Something someone who is hurting says. I wonder if I said the same thing to Matthew.

"It wasn't a true statement? That I'm unlovable?" he asks.

"No," I say.

"I'm not so sure," he says, then takes a final sip of his coffee.

**DATE NUMBER FIVE**

We're in a coffee shop. I drove an hour to get here, north of my home, past Alpine Avenue and all the businesses that clump together like mushrooms: Target, Staples, McDonald's, Costco. Past sprawling farmland where there was nothing but fields of snow and naked trees on the horizon. Through a stretch of road so twisty and turny that I had to slow down to twenty miles an hour while a stream of cars grew behind me. Past a stretch of houses and farms where every two hundred feet there was a giant American flag, somehow flapping in the breeze. Enormous flags, each the size of a garage. It scared me, the patriotism in that stretch.

But I'm here now, in this cozy little café in the middle of nowhere. Everything is wood. The floor, the wall, the ceilings, the table. It's like being in Mother Nature's womb.

He's attractive. He looks like a sailor in his black peacoat and black beanie. He's got thick black glasses, a white beard, ice-blue eyes. He was a chef for twenty-five years, and now he's a cannabis farmer.

We don't know what to say to each other.

"Do you drink coffee this late?" he asks.

"Not usually," I say. "But, hey, this is a special occasion."

"I drank all the vodka back in the day. So I've had enough of that."

"Coffee is good."

We sit. I smile. He smiles. "Did you ever live in California?" I ask. He looks at me, a little confused. "I'm sorry, there's just something in your voice. Your accent. Some kind of California or Colorado swing to it."

"I lived in both California and Colorado." Then he starts to tell me stories of the places he's lived and worked. The grueling hours. Of working in kitchens where no one spoke English and you had to pantomime your way through what you wanted. "I expected everyone to speak Spanish, but it wasn't like that at all. First person I met in a kitchen? He was from Poland."

I imagine the hot kitchen. The eighteen-year-old kid trying to figure out what he needs to do with the pile of potatoes in front of him. My son is seventeen and wants to be a chef, and I'm afraid for him. Not that he couldn't handle a stack of potatoes, but that there's so much sadness, late nights, and excess in being in the restaurant business. I was a server for years, so I've seen and felt the grind of it.

"I was kidnapped by Billy Idol for two days," he says and sips his coffee.

"Well, you can't just stop there. You have to tell me that story."

"It was in LA. Man, that place will suck your soul. I never should've gone there. But I did. It was weird, in the late '80s. You'd go get tacos or something and there was Darryl Hannah or Iggy Pop. You wanted a drink and would go to a bar, and there'd be these famous people, because they want to go to a bar too. I mean, they're really just people, you know? It was surreal. I used to have my grandma send me dirt from home so I could smell it. I missed home so much.

"Anyway, one day I go to a bar to get a vodka tonic and I sit down between these two guys at the bar, and there's no one there. Like no servers. No bartenders. No one. And the three of us just sit there, kinda awkwardly I guess, and it's like, what is this place? Do I just help myself? And then there's all this noise like crashing and shit, and then Billy Idol comes barreling through the swinging doors from the kitchen with like, two women. Guess they were doing coke or something back there. And then he says 'What are ya drinking?' I tell him vodka and he pours me a glass and then we're like instant friends because we're drinking together, and I'm not telling him no. I'm not someone on his team saying he can't do this or that. I'm just enjoying the drink. We drink there for a while and then, somehow, I'm running errands with him. We're just lit, for days, man, and then I'm at his house and it's gross, you know? I mean, not *gross*, like trash and everything. It's gross because this is still the '80s and he had some shit designer and everything was just '80s neon shit or whatever. So I stayed at his house for a few days."

He drinks some more coffee.

"So how did it end? Did you just pick up and leave? What did you do?"

"What did I do? How did it end?" He thinks. "Monday happened. And it was done."

I nod. Drink my coffee. It seems like a lot of good times are killed by Monday. Monday happens all over the place.

He asks me if I want to ditch the coffee and get pizza instead, so we walk across the frozen street, and the pizza is warm and comforting. We chat about things like who we want to be, regret, and how we're both just trying to connect.

The next morning, he removes me as a match from his profile, and he doesn't text me again.

# 24. CHEERS

Three of my girlfriends have organized a Zoom housewarming party for me. I've been in the house for eight months now and no one's seen it except for Erin. The pandemic has affected all of us in so many ways, but it's in these little celebrations where I feel it the most, because what it feels like is rejection. It feels like people haven't seen my home because they don't like me. No one wants to spend time with me. No one cares.

That's not a *true* feeling. It's just a feeling.

My girlfriends chipped in and bought me some gin from a local brewery, simple rosemary syrup, and a bag of grapefruits so I can mix my favorite drink and have martinis with them. Erin dropped the stuff off to me, and I almost cried. I almost-cry a lot, but this was a good one, both because of the organization they put into this, but also because they know my favorite drink is a Greyhound. It's being known that feels so good.

"Shake it up!" Meg says. She's in New York. All my closest friends are narrators and performers. Sometimes I look at them and just can't get over how pretty they are. And smart. And successful. And just plain charming. Before narrating, Meg took care of dogs for famous people. Now she's drinking a glass of wine that is filled to the brim.

Lilith is in LA. She stares into the camera with a hint of defiance. Not that the camera is doing anything to her, it's just her resting face. She rides Harleys and wears leather; she's so cool that when I'm next to her in real life, I sort of want to apologize. She's drinking tequila tonight.

Erin is in her home. She couldn't be here. Her partner wasn't feeling well, so she's staying home and making sure she hasn't contracted Covid. She's got a Captain Morgan and Coke.

I begin to shake the martini shaker. The metal shaker smokes with cold and the ice inside thunks. "Fucking cold!" I say. They encourage me to shake some more. I do, feeling my boobs and my body vibrate and a weird thing starts to happen, I smile. It's so stupid, shaking my whole body in my empty kitchen, while my girlfriends cheer me on. And when I say stupid, I mean wonderful.

I pour the drink in my martini glass, the cute old fashioned one I bought after the divorce that came in a set for all the parties I'd throw. The rest of the glasses are still in a box.

"All right," Lilith says, "Time for a tour!"

I grab my drink in one hand and my computer in the other, and somehow manage to spin around and walk the stairs and talk about the house. I'm sure I'm making them seasick. I'm seasick doing it, and at the same time, I'm joyous. This is the first time I've had people "in" my house, friends' voices here, and there's something about it, something so healing I can feel my heart start to stitch itself back together.

"That fucking bathroom!" Lillith exclaims, "It's huge!"

"It's not," I say. "It's normal size." The bathroom is cute. Black-and-white floor, subway tile in the bath, two showerheads, a window that lets in the light.

"It's HUGE," Meg says. "You forget, I'm in New York and Lilith is in LA. We don't have closets, let alone bathtubs."

"Show them your backyard," Erin says.

I do. Proudly. There are two levels to the deck, and a huge oak tree in the backyard. In another month, everything will be bursting with green. Right now, spring is just starting and there are flowers and buds, birds and squirrels. There are fairy lights on the deck the previous owners left.

"God," Lilith breathes. "It's fucking beautiful."

"Look at this! Look at what you did," Meg says.

Maybe I'm drunk already, or maybe it's just being with friends, but there's something about that idea. Look at what I did. I started over. I built something. I let this house be my life. One day, it's going to be heavy with growing things.

"Yeah," I say. "Just look." I make another drink. We talk about nothing for the next hour or so, and it's lovely. It's so lovely. It's so, so wonderful and light.

# 25. Things Go On

"Let's schedule you for an endocrinologist and see what's going on there," the doctor says. I agree. I agree with joy. Because I'm so tired all the time and how do I go on dating apps and present my best self when I'm losing hair and sleep and confidence?

"Okay," I say.

***

"Let's schedule you weekly for a while," my therapist says. My anxiety has been skyrocketing, and I've been trying to delve deeper into my childhood to see if there's a reason I've had two divorces and I can't seem to connect with anyone long term.

"Okay," I say.

***

"You want to meet in a couple of weeks?" From my life coach.

"Yes, please," I say.

"Maybe we can try some reiki next time."

"Honestly," I say. "I'm up for anything."

***

"What podcasts are you listening to now?" Erin asks.

"I've been listening to Glennon Doyle and Brené Brown. Also, Elizabeth Gilbert's *Big Magic.* You?"

"Same. I'm doing all this work, but I wish he'd listen to the podcasts and do some work too."

I nod. Erin is still struggling with her husband. It seems to me they've reached that point where things are so broken, you can't fix anything. Erin is trying to fix herself, but it's the relationship that's broken, not her.

I'm still trying to fix myself too. Glennon Doyle and Brené Brown make it seem easy: just claim yourself, be rooted, be emotionally open and vulnerable, accountable for your actions, learn the right way to apologize, but it's somehow not enough. I don't feel fixed.

"You know what else I'm listening to?" I ask. "These podcasts on marriage from Ester Perel. They're amazing. She's a therapist and each episode is a session with a married couple who are at a breaking point. And they hash it out and she records it."

"That sounds terrible."

"I mean it is, but it's also interesting. It's like...I don't know...the shit people go through in marriages. What they put up with."

"Does she fix things?"

I think about it. I think about the episodes with the husbands who are serial cheaters. Sometimes it's the wives, but mostly it's the husbands. I think of the women who keep telling their husbands that of course they don't want to have sex with them because their husbands have turned them into a mother. I think of the episodes where the couples talk about anger, distance, numbing, loss, pain, and...

"Fuck," I say, "I don't think she's really helping."

"Is any of this helping?" Erin asks.

"I honestly don't know."

***

That night, I write a letter to the universe talking about the kind of partner I want. My life coach recommended this idea, as did my therapist. Focus on qualities you want, not appearance. I struggle writing this.

Dear Universe,

I want love. I want companionship. I want to be wanted. I want someone who is around my age, who wants to travel, and is kind. He is attracted to me and he likes to spend time with me. We laugh together. He has a good job. He doesn't need me to lift him up, he just wants me to be by his side. He is empathetic. He is communicative. He is a safe place. He wants to be loved.

I look at this letter, and it doesn't seem possible. Not after all I've been through. Not after my life, my upbringing, my marriages, my disappointments. What I know about love is you have to earn it, you have to prove you're worthy of it, and at any moment, all the rules can change and you'll have to convince them you're worth staying for. A man who simply loves you? That doesn't really seem possible. It seems laughable.

I put the letter in my nightstand drawer, next to the unopened condoms and "just in case" KY Jelly.

I leave that letter there, but really, I want to replace it with another letter. I want this letter to say something that's a little simpler:

Dear Universe,

I just want someone to love me back.

# 26. We Meet

It's April and there is still snow, but the sun is out too. I see Ryan pull up in his Honda. It's the same car I have, only a little older and blue instead of burgundy. I try not to look at him, but I can't help it. He looks just like his pictures. Big, kind blue eyes. Taller than me. Trim. And as he walks across the street, I stand up, wave, smile, and then a flush of embarrassment washes over me and I feel my cheeks turn red. He's wearing army green jeans and an orange jacket, and so am I.

"I see you got my memo on the outfit," he says as a greeting.

"Yes. Very kind of you to send that." I'm sure he's disappointed in me. I've had so many disappointments in meeting men that I want to give him an out before we even begin. "Did you still want a coffee?" I ask, but what I'm really asking is, do you want a coffee with me? Are you attracted to me? Am I too heavy, too plain? Is this worth your time? Am I worth your time?

"Coffee, yeah. Of course. Maybe a walk too. You up for that?"

I smile. I nod. There's a vibe about him I like. He seems familiar somehow, but we've only chatted. His texts, though, were kind and inquisitive. I know he has two boys close to my kids' age. He's been divorced a few years. He loves going to Northern Michigan. He's smart. He's acted a bit, done a little vaudeville-style theater so maybe he won't be threatened by my work or my poems or my blogs. Maybe, this is a man who can handle me.

We get our coffee and head back outside and start to walk. The sun in our face. It's so warm that I take off my jacket, a little embarrassed to show my body. The T-shirt is a little tight and it's got a V-neck low enough to expose my cleavage. I hope he's a boob man, because there's just no hiding them for long.

I don't know what we talk about but I know we're both smiling and laughing. Every now and then he touches my arm for emphasis, or to steady me when I almost trip. We walk for twenty minutes or so one way, and I know it'll be twenty minutes back, so I ask if he needs to turn around. He says, "Or maybe we could sit for a while? Chat a bit more if you're up for it?" He only had an hour for our meeting and I am happy he's extending it.

We head out through the trail to the water. There's a dock that bobs through the lake, surrounded by marsh. Last year, a swan nested right off of the dock and terrorized walkers passing by her and her brood. The swan's not there now though.

The water laps gently around us. The sky is a bright blue with thick fluffy clouds. Every now and then the sun shines so bright that I have to squint.

There's a bench at the end of the dock. No fishermen are there now. No one is. So we sit. Our knees touch for a second and I apologize. He smiles.

He asks me questions. About my upbringing. About life. He tells a funny story about his prom date in high school, his most embarrassing moment involving his giant, unrelenting teenage erection, and I laugh with him, for him. I feel the sun warm my chest and I think I might actually get sunburned a little, and how it will be a reminder that for a little while, I sat with someone in the sun and talked and laughed and felt good.

When we walk back to our cars, I am sad to say goodbye. Surely, this is too good to be true. He is a kind man and maybe, probably, he isn't even interested in me. He just slowed down and took some time with a stranger because he said he would.

I know I won't see him again.

But I want to.

Oh, how I want to.

# 27. QUESTIONS

ME: I just wanted to say how much I enjoyed our walk and chat. I have a feeling I'm not quite your type, but it was lovely to meet you.
HIM: Oh? I had a lovely time too. Did I do something or say something that would make you think that you're not my type? It would help me
with meeting people in the future to know if I gave off those vibes. :)
ME: No. Not at all. I just thought...I'm not as fit as you and I just assumed...I thought you were/are really cute and fun and you made me smile.
HIM: You are just my type. You're quirky and cute and I like your style and I liked talking to you. Would you like to get together again?

***

We agree to meet at Panera the next week. Not exactly romantic, but choices are limited. When I pull up, I see him waiting in his car. We get out of our cars and he says, "It's closed, can you believe it? I'm so sorry. It never occurred to me that it would be closed."

"Pandemic living, yeah?"

We stand in the parking lot. Look around. There's a sign on the door that says CLOSED TEMPORARILY. I wonder how long TEMPORARILY is. Maybe Temporary is really Forever. The spring sun of last week has faded and it's cold and wintry again. Too cold for a walk.

We look up and down 28th Street. Lots of businesses. Lots of closed stores. It's 9:00 a.m. and not many things are open. Not many places are open even when it's not 9:00 a.m.

Ryan scratches his face. "Want to chat in one of our cars?" There's a slight pause and then he says, "I don't want to make you uncomfortable, but I also don't want to cancel. If we can make some space to talk, I'd love to."

I invite him into my car. We sit in the parking lot and chat. It feels a little reckless, being maskless and talking, and it also feels wonderfully normal.

"I brought some questions," he says.

"Oh. You brought them? Like you wrote them down?"

He laughs nervously. "Well, yeah. I was kinda thinking about things I wanted to ask you so I made a list." He unfolds a sheet of paper from his pocket.

"Oh. Look at that. You typed it and everything!" I can't help but laugh a little.

"Is this weird? It's a little weird, isn't it?"

"I like it," I say, because I do. I snuggle in. He smooths the sheet of paper out and I am mentally preparing to dive in and unfurl the hurts of my upbringing. I don't want to talk about my dad and how he checked out. I don't want to talk about my mom and how *she* checked out. I don't want to talk about pain, loneliness, confusion; or abandonment, hurt, my past marriages, disappointments, where I went wrong, where they went wrong, where we failed...but this is what you do when you're getting to know someone. You ask tough questions. You tell your history, then, and only then, can you get to the good stuff, to the actual fun of being together. I think, maybe, I can trust him with these tender truths of mine. There's something about him. Something in his eyes, or the way he gently touches my arm when he's making a point.

But what he asks instead surprises me. "How do you think you're going to die?"

There's an actual moment of cognitive dissonance. My brain does the record scratch thing. "Huh?" I say, and then I laugh. Not what I was expecting at all.

"That's a heavy one to start with. Maybe one of the others? Do you believe in aliens and if so, do you think they've had interaction here on earth?"

"These are your questions?"

"Well, yeah." He smiles. "I thought it would be fun to know some things about you."

"I was expecting you'd ask where I grew up and what my diet preferences are."

"Do you want to talk about that?"

I think, and respond naturally: "No. Actually, I don't want to talk about that. I'd like to know if you believe in Bigfoot. Please note, your answer should be yes. And I'd also like to know if you've ever watched *Laurence Welk*."

"I record it."

"You're fucking kidding me."

"No. I love *Lawrence Welk*. It's really..."

"Comforting," I say. "It's all those sequins."

"The polyester is good too," he says.

Then we talk for an hour or so. No coffee. No food. Just us in my car. Cars zooming up and down 28th Street, just in front of us. Snow starts to fall softly outside and I think that maybe this parking lot is romantic after all. Eventually, he looks at his watch. "Maybe we could do this again? Only in an actual restaurant?" he asks.

"Yes," I say, "But only if you bring some more questions."

# 28. Love at First Sight

"Do you believe in love at first sight?"

Erin looks at me over her gyro and does an eye roll so epic, I think teenagers would be jealous. "Fuck no," she says.

"Maybe just a little? Maybe not love, exactly, but maybe something else? Something like home?"

"You're asking me if I believe in home at first sight? Are we talking hypothetically or for real?"

"I don't know."

"The answer is the same. Fuck no."

I nod. Take a bite of my spinach pie. The phyllo flakes everywhere. I want to sprinkle the flakes with salt and just lick them up. I look at Erin. She shrugs. I grab the salt shaker.

"You're not talking hypothetically, are you? Who was the guy you met again?"

I tell her his name.

"The *Lawrence Welk* dude? That's Ryan?"

I nod.

"You feel like you're in love with him?"

When she says it, it sounds crazy. I recognize that.

"Of course I'm not in love with him. That's ridiculous. We've had two dates. A walk and a weird coffee in our cars in the parking lot of Panera."

"I dunno. I think I hear wedding bells..."

"Stop it. I'm not in love with him, but, you know, I can see things."

"Dead people? Do you see dead people?"

"It's a good thing I'm old. I can still get your references. No. I see a potential future with this guy. He's...it's hard to explain. He's really awkward and cute and disarming. He's real. I'm attracted to him. He makes me laugh."

"Have you kissed him? Has he kissed you? In the parking lot of Panera?"

"No."

"He's probably gay."

"He's not gay!"

"How do you know?"

"Because I felt it."

"You felt it? You felt his dick in the parking lot of Panera?" She is mock-shocked.

"No!" And I am exasperated. I mean, it's funny and I sort of laugh a little but then I stop. "I felt like there could be potential with this one, and I don't know what to do about it."

"What's there to do? You go with it. You see him again. You kiss him. Check out his package. See if you'll fit."

"We'll fit. I know it."

And then we both laugh because I'm not exactly sure if we're talking about sex, love, relationships, or what.

Erin pushes her plate away. "It doesn't matter, really, does it? You're laughing. I haven't heard you laugh in a long time. And for that, I like this guy."

"Yeah," I say. "Me too."

# 29. The Things We Do

We go for a long walk. We get takeout. We cook together. He comes over to my house. I go over to his.

He texts me every morning: How are you? What's your day like? How are you feeling today?

I text him back. I start to share my writing with him, my tiny poems, my blogs. I send him this:

My lips want
to taste you
but if I lean forward
and you pull away
I'll be left
suspended
and what will I do then
f l o a t i n g
in the space between
Us?

He says: Does this mean I should kiss you?

I say: Yes.

We meet at a dingy bar by his house because it's the only thing that's open on a Thursday night at eight. I drink a G&T and he has an IPA. We talk about our kids, our goals, aliens (again), the economy, what's happening in the world, how we have all lost the ability to connect, how recovering from divorce is so hard, so painful, so confusing. We talk until they start flipping chairs over on tables, and the waitress gives us The Look.

Outside, it is dark and quiet. The street lamps buzz. He kisses me in the cocoon of golden light. It is not a great kiss. It is nervous. Tentative. Afraid. But there is something there. Some kind of energy. When he pulls back from kissing me, he pats my butt and smiles, and I know it will only get better from here.

Days pass. We text.

I liked kissing you.

I liked it too.

I want to kiss you again.

Me too.

When?

Where?

Soon.

He comes over to my house.

We make risotto with fresh leeks and peas, topped with shrimp. He chops the garlic; I stir the risotto. We move in the kitchen with an easy grace that I never had with either of my husbands.

We chat here and there. In between the chatting there is silence, but it is not the silence of having nothing to say. It's the silence of having said enough.

He touches my hips when he passes behind me.

We taste the risotto. A spoon for him. A spoon for me.

We eat outside on my back porch where it's finally, beautifully spring. It is green, green, green. Purple, red, and white flowers bloom around us. The world is vibrant and alive. I didn't know I had so many flowers in my yard. I am so grateful.

We chat and laugh. He wiggles a little when he tastes the risotto.

The music floats through the screen window and surrounds us and the risotto is perfect, the shrimp plump, the wine cool and crisp.

My kids are at their dad's so the house is mine, the time is mine, the space is mine, and I think that maybe Ryan is mine too.

Later, when we undress, he looks me in the eyes for a few moments and we just hold. We just hold the moment, vulnerable, naked, alive, looking at each other. The next time he kisses me, there is no awkwardness or fear or trepidation. There is only want, desire, and beneath that a comfort I was not expecting, an ease.

It is not great sex, but it is good. There is potential here. Maybe I can give him a few pointers. It is satisfying though, to be with him, and it is easy to let my mind spin forward and think of all the good things that are finally going to happen. With me. With him. With us.

Afterward, he asks if he can hold me, and so I curl in next to him. He wraps his arms around me, one of his hands on my breast. We are shaped like two S's next to each other. Our breathing aligns. He kisses my shoulder and says, "Thank you."

I want to cry. Not from sadness, of course, but for the feeling of being connected. Of being seen. Of being wanted.

It has been so long since I felt those things. It isn't that I'd forgotten the feeling of being wanted and connected; it's I didn't believe that was something I would ever feel again.

I feel it now.
Next to him.
And then we both laugh.
For no reason at all.

# 30. Doctor Visits

"So your blood work shows you have high cortisol levels."

"Cortisol level is related to stress, right?"

"Yes."

"Makes sense."

"But you also have high levels of DHEA sulfate."

"And what's that mean?"

"It means there's maybe something going on with your adrenal glands. So we're going to prescribe a small dose of dexamethasone to you, and we'll have you check back in another three months."

"I mean, okay, but I have to wait another three months? To see if there's an issue? But doesn't the blood test say that there's an issue? I mean, there must be an issue if you're prescribing something."

"There's maybe an issue, but if the dexamethasone alleviates some of the symptoms, then we'll move on from there."

I should be happy to know something, but this *something* is so vague that I don't understand it or what it means, if anything.

And then I have a mammogram that comes back suspicious. So I go back the following day—it's scary how fast they have me come in—for another check and the whole time I'm thinking: "It's cancer. Of course, it's cancer. Because this is my life. My life is hard and there is no relief and I am going to die. I'll die and my kids will be left without me, and how is this even fair? How is this good? I am doing all the work. I am trying so hard to be good, kind, loving, and vulnerable and how do I handle this? I have two thousand dollars in my checking account, and I don't have enough gigs in the summer to pay all the bills, let alone additional medical bills. I can't afford to be sick. I can't afford to take two weeks off. And who is going to drive me to appointments? Who do I list as my emergency contact person? I don't have parents, I don't have family, so who do I list to call if I flatline in the office or something?"

I know, of course, I can list Erin, but this seems to go above and beyond what a friend should do. What I need is family. And I don't have family, and I am running out of time. There are so many things I want to do, and my boobs are going to ruin everything.

***

My boobs end up being fine.

I have extremely dense tissue and it's hard for them to read the mammogram. I should come back every year. Get tested every year.

I'm not dying right now, I guess. So, I have time...to fix my life?

But I can feel my cortisol levels rising, I can feel my hair falling out, I can feel myself floating because besides my kids and a few close friends, I don't have anyone who holds me to this earth. I don't have anyone for my kids to call if I need help.

# 31. Exclusive

Ryan and I have been dating for a few weeks now. Lots of texts in between seeing each other. I'm looking forward to getting dressed up and going out with him, especially since more and more things are opening up, but his schedule is pretty packed. Next weekend, he's taking his kids on a road trip down Route 66. They're going to stop at all the quirky places along the way.

This is something I've always wanted to do. I love kitsch and road trips. Part of me envisions in a year or so, his kids and mine, us renting a big RV for some kind of road trip. It feels good to think about, but I have to remind myself that all of this is just starting and I don't really know where any of this will end up.

We are in his living room. His cat is on my lap, and I'm sitting next to Ryan. There's a faint smell of cat litter in the air and his house is dusty. Definitely a bachelor's space. "I'm so sorry about the cat box," he says, and then opens a window behind us.

"It's okay," I say. But I think of giving him the name of a cleaning lady. He just needs some help organizing his life a little bit. "So you'll be gone for a week and a half?"

"Yep. I'm going to text you from the trip, if that's okay, send you pictures?"

I'm delighted by this idea. "Yes! Please! I want to see all the things."

"It'll be nice to have you to talk to. Sort of like you're coming along with me. It's going to be rough doing it all on my own with the boys." He'll have long days of driving, of keeping them all fed, of intervening in the boys' spats. He'll be exhausted. I have been through the same with my kids. It's hard sometimes, when you're on your own.

"I know," I say. "Single parenting is rough, but what an amazing trip." I think of the week and a half without seeing him and I say without thinking, "I'll miss you."

He smiles, reaches for my hands, and then kisses me. "I'll miss you too." He takes a breath. "I've been thinking about something and I'm wondering how you would feel if we were exclusive?"

He smiles again and it is tentative. He is nervous and it is darling. My heart is warm.

"You want to be exclusive with me? Just me and you?" I ask. Just to clarify. Because I feel hope, and it scares me. Maybe I misunderstood.

"Just me and you. Would you be okay with that?"

"Yeah! Of course. Just me and you." I like the phrase. It fits.

I smile and kiss him. It feels like he's about to give me his letterman jacket.

"And I have another question," he says. "It's a little awkward, but if you had to choose, how many times would you make love in a week?"

The question startles me a little, but it also feels really adult. Matt and I never talked about our expectations and maybe this was where we went wrong. We never talked about what we wanted in sex really, or how often. And we were both constantly disappointed. I think about how he'd reach for me at ten at night, and by that time, I was already too tired. *Reach for me at 8:30*, I'd wanted to say. And then he stopped reaching for me at all, and I stopped encouraging him. How many times would I like to make love? I don't really know, so I say, "Oh, about once a week, I guess."

He's still smiling but there's something a little different about it now.

"What about you?" I ask. "How many times would you make love with your *exclusive partner*?" I giggle a little at the phrase 'exclusive partner.' This is such an awkward conversation.

"Once a day, really, but I'd settle for three to four times a week."

"Oh," I say. Then he starts to kiss me and I want to change my answer. I want to say, I didn't know once a day was a possibility, but instead we just kiss, and I think, I'm exclusive with this man. He and I are together. And our wild adventure together is just beginning.

# 32. Walking

Erin and I start walking together three times a week. It feels hardcore. We want to get in shape, lose weight, but more than that, we're both so incredibly anxious that the only thing that seems to help besides martinis, is walking. So, we walk. Around Reed's Lake. Four-point-five miles. A little longer if we meander through the neighborhoods.

Erin's marriage isn't going great. He's not trying. It would be easy for him to try, but he doesn't seem to want to. It's like he's just checked out. Emotionally he's out the door, usually he's physically out the door too. We talk about that. We talk about loneliness. There is the loneliness of being alone, but there is also the loneliness of being in a relationship when your person no longer sees you, and that is maybe a worse kind of loneliness. It's a loneliness that erases you slowly over time.

"I don't want to talk about it," she says. She picks up the pace.

"You're walking really fast."

"I know. I'm sorry. I don't want to talk about it, but I'm too mad to slow down."

I move my short legs a little faster. I'm like a centipede trying to keep up with her, my legs moving in a blur.

"Tell me more about this guy," she says, changing the subject.

"He has a name."

"I know, but until I meet him, I'm not sure we should name him."

"You mean we shouldn't name him until I'm sure he's going to stick around. I don't disagree with you."

"Is he coming to your party?"

I'm throwing a housewarming/work party, even though I've been in my home for almost a year. "He is but..."

"Uh oh."

"No. No uh oh. The week before, he's taking his boys on a trip. They're doing the whole Route 66 thing. He'll get back on the day of my party and then come over for a bit."

"Won't he be exhausted?"

"He will, but he knows it's important to me, so he said he'll be there."

"I like that."

"I do too."

"But didn't he just get back from a different trip?"

"He did. He travels a lot."

"But hasn't he been traveling, like every weekend since you met and that's why he hasn't taken you out on the weekend? Why you only meet on Thursdays or whatever?"

I slow down. Motion to stop. I can't breathe. I can't keep up. "Gimme a minute," I say. I bend down to tie my shoe, even though it doesn't need tying. Something is niggling at me.

"I'm just saying...you sure about this? Like, you're sure you're not a Tuesday Girl to him?"

I stand up quickly and my head spins a little. I'm dizzy. "Whoa, there," Erin says and reaches out. I grab hold of her until it passes.

Am I a Tuesday Girl? It's a story I told Erin about. About how there's a pattern in my life of choosing men who aren't really into me, who only want me around occasionally, but not long term, never on the weekend. They just want to see me when a hole opens up in their schedule.

This can't be true. It's not true. This is different. The potential between me and him is huge. I feel grounded when we're together. We have an ease with one another. The sex is good. The conversation better. We just discussed going exclusive and our expectations with intimacy. This is a man who is into me. I know it without question.

But he's never taken me out on the weekend. We've never gone to a restaurant. When I've asked him to go up north or to Chicago, he said he wished he could but he was traveling with his sons, or to visit his family, or having a weekend with his friends. There just hasn't been time or space. He's coming back in a week and a half, and we haven't made any plans to see each other besides him stopping by the party.

He has a lot on his mind though. This is a big trip he's taking with his two teenagers. We'll discuss details when he gets back.

Erin and I start walking again. "I know for you that sex validates you. It makes you feel like you're in a relationship, but his actions aren't saying that. There's something up with this guy," she says.

I don't feel like talking anymore.

When I go home, I start thinking about The Tuesday Girl.

Maybe I'll write about it.

# 33. The Party

"I'm so nervous," I say.

"I can tell. You've organized those straws five times. Just put them in a fucking cup."

I look down at the pack of straws in my hands. Erin grabs them, puts them in a red Solo cup, and sets them on the counter. "What if no one comes?" I ask.

"They're going to come. You've already had RSVPs from a dozen people. They're coming."

"Okay, so then, what if they all come?"

"You can handle this. Your house looks great. There's plenty of food. You said it was a potluck so there will be even more food. They're going to come."

I go through the RSVP list in my head and try to think logically. I've made ham and cheese sliders, there's chips and dips, fruit, charcuterie, and Erin brought stuff for root beer floats. There's wine and booze and beer. If everyone comes and no one brings anything, there will still be enough food. I'm so excited to have people in my house. This is what I've dreamed of. A home filled with laughter and music and friends, something I could never have when I was with Matthew. We had one party in our decade together and that was in the beginning, before depression took hold and we fell apart. All of this is so fun, so I don't understand why I'm so nervous.

"I think I've forgotten how to people," I say.

Erin grabs the gin, the grapefruit juice, and the martini shaker. "God, ain't that the truth. I haven't seen anyone in, what, a year and a half? What are we going to talk about?"

"I don't know. And I don't even know how to start. I mean, to anyone, really, if you ask how are you, it's going to be the same answer. There's a fucking pandemic happening and I haven't been outside in over a year. Things are fucked."

"Things are fucked. Greyhound?" she asks. I nod.

We drink.

***

People do come, of course. I think we're all a little leery about being inside, even though the windows are open and there's a nice breeze. But my backyard is comfortable and alive with growing things and the scent of flowers in the wind. The table bows with the old-fashioned potluck bounty. There's an actual casserole of some kind, a quinoa salad, so many cookies, cake, taco dip, and mozzarella and tomato kabobs on little plastic swords.

Everyone here is a narrator and their lush voices float in the air along with the music. "A fucking potluck!" Caitlin says by way of greeting. She stands triumphantly, a bottle of wine in each hand. She's so excited that I sort of wonder if she's going to drop to her knees and tear off her shirt like she just made a winning goal.

"Caitlin!" I cry. She hugs me. And it is a great hug. A hug that isn't just being kind. A hug that connects.

"I am so happy to see you," she says, her eyes watery.

I nod because words are hard.

Julie comes with her partner, and Tom and Charlotte (both narrators) arrive with booze and fruit. Sadie is here, and Frank, and Mel. These are my colleagues and my friends and I can't...

I can't process.

Happiness is so foreign that it hurts. This is my home and my friends are here with me, in my home, in person, and we are all shimmery drunk and happy.

The sun is strong and warm on us, even though it's already six o'clock.

I told the kids they needed to come down and talk to people for a few minutes. "Just until we have a toast, and then you can go back to your rooms."

My son works the crowd. He's got that James Spader smoothness to him and I worry a little bit about what that could mean. He chats with different people, asks them questions, listens, shakes hands. And I wonder who is this social child, and what happened to my regular withdrawn sixteen-year-old?

My daughter struggles a bit more. I can see the anxiety flooding her, so I give her a job of cutting the cookie-brownies. "You better taste one, just to make sure it's edible," I suggest.

She gladly tries them out. "I better taste two," she says. "Just to be sure the first one wasn't a fluke."

As we pour the champagne into plastic flutes, my *Lawrence Welk* man shows up. Ryan hugs me and kisses me in front of everyone, and he's smiling. A smile so big it lights him from the inside out.

"I just got home," he says. "Literally. I haven't even showered."

"I don't care! I'm so glad you're here. You must be exhausted!"

He looks tired. He nods a little and holds my hand. He can't stay long, I know, and it's a lot for me to expect. But he is here. He kept his word. And he kissed me in front of everyone. He's not embarrassed by me. We are together and that is enough.

We pass out the champagne flutes. My daughter has lemonade and my son asks if he can have the champagne. I agree because he is sixteen and it is summer and my friends are here and I am in love with being alive. We raise our glasses. "I'm not exactly sure what to say," I start, and I just look at everyone for a moment. How different everyone is. Our skin colors, our ages, our genders. What we wear, our voices. We are so different, but we share the same occupation, and somehow, this connects us on a deeper level. I'm overwhelmed. "To each other!" I manage to say, my heart full. Tears in my eyes.

"To us!"

***

Later, Ryan and I text. He can't get together this weekend because he has a writing retreat with his sketch comedy buddies. Then the following week, he is getting together for two weeks with his sister and her family. But he could meet me this week on Tuesday night. Maybe he could come over and we could 'be together.' He means have sex, of course. A drink maybe, but mostly, he wants to have sex.

It bothers me that he only has Tuesdays available, after golf, and he can come over, but he can't take me out. I agree anyway. It's something. He's fitting me into his life, and isn't that lovely? Isn't that what you do when you date? You compromise. You make it work.

Tuesday it is.

# 34. THE TUESDAY GIRL

Throughout my life, writing has always been a way for me to understand things. It helps me to put feelings and experiences into words. Words make my emotions and experiences 3-D, so I can look at things from a bit of a distance and understand.

Something is eating at me. Not eating at me really, it's more like a flutter inside my stomach that is curious and telling me to sit down and write. There's something worrying me about dating Ryan, my wants and needs, and I can't quite figure it out.

When he mentioned he could get together on Tuesday, I tried not to let it hurt. But it did.

Erin had mentioned the Tuesday Girl thing to me, and I decide to blog about it. Ryan is making time to be with me, but it's only here and there. I'm confused because you should see someone regularly if you're exclusive. And he mentioned he liked to have sex every day, but would settle for three or four, but we are barely even seeing each other once a week. Something is wrong. I know it.

Dating as an adult is hard. There's so little space when kids, work, and responsibilities fight for attention.

When I sit down to write, it pours out of me. I'm surprised by what I write and discover. I decide it's important. There's something here that I need to share, and I'm not sure why or how exactly. But this needs to be out there.

So, I post it to my blog. What is worrying me with Ryan is, even though on the surface of things I seem important to him and he tells me I'm important to him, something isn't aligning. It feels off, like a picture hanging on a wall that is slightly askew. You don't really notice what's wrong with it, but you feel it.

I write about being a Tuesday Girl.

When I post it, I receive so many responses from other women who have also been a Tuesday Girl that I'm surprised and saddened. There are so many of us. I really hope I'm wrong this time. I don't want to be a Tuesday Girl again.

THE TUESDAY GIRL

Blog

When I lived in New York, shortly after 9/11, I met a man who I fell head over heels for. Maybe I was extra vulnerable after that terrible day, or because I was still new to the city, or maybe it was just that I was in my twenties and healed enough from my childhood to be ready to love. I was heart-open ready to love. I fell for him pretty instantly.

It didn't last long.

He wasn't into me or ready for me or whatever. I believed though, if I were just patient enough, loving enough, understanding enough, he'd see me as a great partner. He'd change his mind.

I remember one night when we were supposed to meet after he had an event, at like 8 o'clock. He didn't show. I can't remember the exact phone call or text, but he said he was on his way and to just wait.

So I did. Outside his apartment in the dark in Brooklyn. It was November, and I waited. And then it started to rain. It was cold. And I waited. I was drenched, but he said he was coming, and I couldn't let him down. The doorman watched me and after a half hour or so, he asked if I wanted to come inside and wait. I said no, don't worry, he'll be here any minute.

He did show up. Around ten. He felt terrible. He didn't realize he was so late, or that it was raining. He forgot I'd been waiting for him.

The point here is, though, he wasn't thinking of me at all. And that's the part I didn't understand. I wasn't important to him. I didn't even cross his mind.

I still think about that night. The length I was willing to go to, to get the man I was in love with to show up and be there for me. I'd go through anything for him. Even standing in the rain for over an hour, wet and bone chilled. It's still humiliating.

I'd like to say this was a one-time thing, but I'm afraid it's become a pattern.

*

After my first divorce, I connected with a man I'd known for ages.

He invited me over to his house to watch shows. He invited a lot of women over to watch movies and shows, and I suspect he still does, but for some reason I thought I was special.

Naturally, our movie watching evolved. We never slept together...but there was an intensity and a growing bond. Only he could never see me on the weekends. Only on Tuesdays. He was super busy with work and his family and there just wasn't time to get together then, but there would be soon, maybe, and he'd see me on the next Tuesday. And weren't our Tuesdays great?

I agreed because I could empathize with work and family and obligations.

Until I realized it wasn't true.

There was a weekend he was out of town at a family reunion, and he'd been tagged on Facebook in the pictures from the weekend. Only it wasn't a family reunion. They were pictures of him and the woman he was living with, or marrying or whatever, and her two kids.

I was dumbfounded. I had no idea. None at all.

I felt duped and embarrassed, and then it got worse.

He invited me out for cocktails. I was thrilled because we never went out, and I thought he was going to explain those pictures, and maybe he was starting to love me because he'd finally asked me out. I got dressed up and met him at a local restaurant, so excited and happy to be out with him on a date. An actual date! And he said the woman he was involved with had told him he couldn't see anyone else so he was sorry, but we weren't going to have our Tuesdays anymore.

He asked me how I was. I looked at my half-empty martini and I literally did not know what to say. I'd dressed up for this. I'd had this foolish kind of hope that I was special. This wasn't a date at all. The reason we were in a restaurant was because he didn't want me to cause a scene. He didn't want to deal with my emotions. So I left. The drink. Him. The situation.

AND THEN IT GOT WORSE.

I saw the woman at Target the next weekend. She was there with her two kids and they were getting supplies for a barbecue. I was there with my two kids, who were about the same age as hers. I heard her talking to her kids in the aisle saying the things they were getting to bring home to the man I'd been seeing. I had this surreal moment of a soft kind of anger. An awareness that we were the same age, with two kids the same age. Both of us artists. So why was I the Tuesday Girl? Why wasn't I good enough to be the Forever Girl?

And what made this guy so special that he was allowed to decide who was worthy?

It's something that's followed me around, this curse of feeling somehow I am never quite enough, or I'm always a bit much.

I vowed I'd never be a Tuesday Girl again.

*

Of course, it's happened again.

I've been seeing a man on and off who I feel a deep connection with, but who, ultimately, isn't ready or willing or enamored enough to really want me. He sees me maybe once a week. He texts me, he's kind to me, but he's so distant, and there are so many rules to the relationship. He tells me he's not ready yet, and what I hear is "Just give me more time. Be patient." But what he's really saying is: "I don't want you to be my girlfriend."

I've seen him on other days besides Tuesdays, but it may as well be just Tuesdays. We've tried so hard to make it work, but when I look at the relationship AS IT IS, the truth is, he just doesn't want me. I'm not a Forever Girl for him.

Worse than that, though, is I allowed myself to be a Tuesday Girl again. I allowed it. And this isn't going to change, until I change it.

WHO IS A TUESDAY GIRL?

A Tuesday Girl never takes priority. She's not worth enough to spend a weekend with, or make plans with. She's the person a man calls when they have space in their schedule, or downtime, or they're bored, and usually it's last minute. A Tuesday Girl is on the outskirts of the week and priorities and plans. A Tuesday Girl doesn't complain and she's always available and compliant and understanding. She supports. She dreams. She's always available. A Tuesday Girl doesn't express her own needs, because they aren't important. He is the only one who is important. His needs matter.

A Tuesday Girl shrinks her own needs until those needs are small enough that she can convince herself that what she receives is enough.

*

For months, I've been standing in the rain, on a Tuesday, thinking if I'm patient enough, supportive enough, or loving enough, he will think I'm worthy enough of loving.

And of course, I am worthy enough of loving.

I shouldn't have to prove it.

***

Later that night, Ryan texts: "I read your blog. You are so important to me. You're not a Tuesday Girl. It couldn't be farther from the truth."

I'm so relieved to hear this. I knew I was overthinking things. I sleep well that night. But the blog stays up.

# 35. More Walking

I can tell even before she gets out of the car that she is not okay. "Oh, God, Erin? What happened?"

She shakes her head. She's already crying. "Let's walk first."

I follow her.

It's a sporadic pace. We walk past the middle school, around the corner then turn left at the tennis courts. The area we are in is really wealthy. We're just visitors here. We go past the big houses that look so perfect, filled with people who also look perfect, but I wonder what's going on inside them, both the houses and people. I'm learning there are cracks and fissures in everything. Sometimes, they're just invisible.

It is not until we've gone down the hill and started walking on the boardwalk through the swamp that she starts to talk. "We're not working on things anymore," she said.

"Christ. Okay. What does that mean? You're done with therapy?"

"I'm not done. But he is. He won't go anymore."

"Okay. So, are you okay with that?"

"I'm fine with it. It'll be hard to do therapy if he's in New York. He's moving. He's decided he wants to be a film actor. So he's packing up everything and moving out."

"Wait. What? I can't, I don't, I don't know how to unpack that statement."

"Right? He's fucking fifty-four years old and he works in a factory. Now he's going to quit everything and go be an actor? It's almost like he's angry at me for being a narrator. Jealous or something. And honestly, if you're going to have a midlife crisis you buy a new car or fucking fuck your secretary or something, but no, he's got to go beyond that. He's got to leave everything. He's got to leave me. Apparently, he doesn't want to fix us. He just wants out."

"And why New York? You go there for Broadway or some shit. Shouldn't he go to LA?"

"Yes. If he was thinking. But his brain left him a long time ago. Say, five years ago when our relationship started going down the toilet. I mean, I knew it. I knew it. I just didn't want to see it. But you know, right? You know how it is. You just justify everything away. Oh, he's with his friends more because he's so stressed out. He doesn't want me to come with him because it's just a guys' night. A guys' weekend. A guys' trip to Florida. I noticed too that as things got better with my career, as I achieved more and got more gigs, he stopped supporting me. He didn't want to hear about my success, so I stopped talking about it. It's like they say in all the books we've read, I got smaller so that he could feel bigger. I understand. I get it. Maybe he was threatened. Maybe we need our space sometimes. Being a couple is exhausting. Sometimes, you just want to be your own person. And I get it. I fucking get it.

"You know what though? All of that is a lie. It isn't because I emasculated him or anything. It's just that he's tired. He just doesn't want to be married anymore. He said he hasn't been happy in years and he just doesn't want to try anymore. He's tired of trying. He wants to be free. Fucking free.

"You go be free, bucko. See how fun it is. I've been pretty much supporting him all these years. It's like you and Matthew, right? You made double the income and you took on the expenses and whatever. And you did it gladly. You did it because you loved him. While he figured his shit out and went from job to job to job and..."

"We're not really talking about me here, though, right?"

"No. We're talking about me. But goddammit. Goddammit!"

I want to stop walking, pull her to me and hug her. Her grief is all encompassing. Her grief throbs. To an outsider, she might look angry. To her partner, she looks enraged, maybe violent, but I know her well enough to know what she really feels is pain. It hurts her so much she can only express it as anger.

"And I think the worst thing is I'm questioning everything now. Did we have the kind of relationship I thought? Did he ever love me? Did he tell me the truth about anything? Or has he just been cruel all these years. If he knew years ago, fucking five years ago, that he was so unhappy, why didn't he fucking tell me? Why did he let me believe what we had was fixable? What the fuck has been happening these last years? Our whole relationship? What is real? What the fuck is real?"

For me, leaving Matthew was a relief. And I wonder if over the years I lied to him too. I think I was cruel to him. I gave him false hope. Why did I do that? Was there a reason for it? For me, I think, I lied not to hurt him or pull him into a fantasy, I lied because I wanted to believe we could be happy. I wanted to think we were good enough together to be happy. Really, it was me I lied to.

But I also lied to him. It's shitty, the person you can become if you're not careful.

"When is he leaving?" I ask.

"Next month. He's leaving in a month. And so now, I have to live in this terrible limbo of going home and he is there, and all our things are there. All our memories. All the good times, like ghosts hanging out in every room. There are all the ghosts of us, and then there's the real us, the now us, and I'm going to have to live in this soup all month, knowing he hates me so much he's going to move to the other side of the country and live a new life without me in it. He's going to be happy."

"You'll be happy to," I say weakly. She looks at me. "You will!"

"Are you?"

I don't have to think about it. "Maybe no one is happy. Maybe not really."

"Fucking life, man," she says.

"Yeah. Fucking life. It's stupid."

"It's so dumb."

"I hate life."

"Life is ugly. I want to kick life in the shins."

"I want to punch life in the throat. The bitch."

"Yeah. Fuck that bitch. Fuck that dick. Fuck *him.*" And then Erin stops. She just stops.

That's when I grab her and hug her, at the bottom of a great hill by the big rock, where walkers part around us. Someone on a bike whizzes past. Birds sing from above.

We just hold on to each other.

What else can you do?

We just hold on.

# 36. Building Things

I bought a garden box because I decided this is a house where things will grow. Only now I'm in the backyard with some shovels and a box from Amazon that's been busted open and I'm looking at all the pieces around me and yet again, I wonder just how the fuck did I get here.

Even easy things are still hard.

I start to unwrap the long plastic boards and lay out the skeleton of the garden box. I'm confused by the diagram to put it together, and just can't seem to make sense of how these separate pieces are going to click and make a garden box with nine different sections for tomatoes, lettuce, basil, and whatever else my heart desires: passion in one box, companionship in another, laughter in two sections.

It makes no sense and I'm frustrated.

"What are you doing?" my daughter calls from the deck.

"I'm growling," I say. I focus on the directions next to me and am overwhelmed by the cellophane, the cardboard, the strips of white plastic. I'm so focused, I don't notice my daughter has joined me. She takes the diagram from me, studies it, studies the piles of stuff around me, and then quietly begins to sort it.

Suddenly, it starts to make sense. It's like one of those Magic Eye pictures when at first all you see is shapes and forms, and then your brain clicks and you can see the hidden object buried in the chaos. My daughter, at fifteen, is clearly a genius.

"How did you do that?" I ask, delighted.

"Mom. It's easy. It's all right there in the drawing."

I still don't see it. "Give me a hand, will you?"

For the next ten minutes, just ten minutes instead of what would've taken me hours, we line up the boards and clip them into place. I tear up the grass while my daughter puts the final dividers into place and then we drag the garden box over the bare earth. "Gosh that's pretty," I say.

"What are you going to do now?" she asks.

"Get piles and piles of dirt. Want to come to the garden center with me?"

"Not particularly." She pauses. Looks around. It occurs to me she probably came out here for a reason.

"Did you want something?" I ask. "I'll make lunch but probably not for an hour or so."

"Oh. Yeah. I just wanted to tell you that I'm non-binary. My pronouns are they and them. And my name is Locust. Okay?"

I think I say, "Uhhhhhh."

I blink a few times. My brain is whirring but I am lost. I was prepared for her being a lesbian. That makes sense to me. I was prepared for transgender. But a single person being a them, being a plural? Non-binary? What does that even mean? And Locust? Locust is Biblical. Locust is like the plague, and this is my sweet girl standing before me who just helped me build a box for things to grow in. None of this makes sense. I laugh a little, and then a little more.

"Couldn't you at least be Cricket? I mean, Cricket I understand."

There is so much she—they—tell me with a look that I'm a little ashamed.

"Forget it," she says. *They* say. Shit. And then they walk away.

I feel like crying. I don't know what I'm supposed to do or say or feel, but surely, it's not this. Surely what I feel shouldn't be pain.

I'm so proud of her. Them. For trusting me. For taking the risk. And I'm really sure I fucked everything up. I said the really wrong thing. But what's happening inside of me is a gentler sorrow. When she was growing in my belly, I only ever called her one name and it wasn't Locust. It wasn't the name of an insect.

My phone buzzes. She's texted me. "You should know that Locust is also a tree."

I start to laugh then.

And cry a little bit.

I sit on the lush green grass next to the newly built garden box and think maybe there is room for one more thing to grow. And maybe that one more thing is me.

# 37. Locust

This time, I'm talking to my aunt. It is bright outside and I'm trying to get my ten minutes of Vitamin D. My doctor says to get Vitamin D from the sun; my dermatologist tells me to cover up. Who the fuck cares? Really, I just want the heat on my skin.

I told my aunt the story of Locust and what I said. I'm surprised by the shame I feel. Not that I have a kid who is non-binary, but by my resistance to the name change, and the pronouns, and letting go of the child I thought I had and replacing her with someone new.

"They've stopped talking to me and when I look at them," I say. "The pain is so sharp it feels like a physical thing between us. She is not a she and she is not the name I gave her. They are their own person, and when they told me their truth, I laughed."

"There are lots of reasons we laugh, honey, and not all of them are because something is funny."

"Right? I was so uncomfortable. I've done all this research and I'm still uncomfortable. I just don't understand why it's important to declare your gender. Wear what you want. Be who you want. Why do you have to declare anything?"

My aunt is silent for a moment. This is where her training as a therapist comes through. She's waiting for me to fill the space. She doesn't have to say anything. The realization comes from me. "Maybe it's more complicated than that," I say. "Maybe there's more to it?"

"Maybe," she agrees. "What if you wrote them a letter? I know you think and process through words and that might give both of you some space to figure this out."

"A letter? Who writes letters anymore?" But I like the idea. I warm up to it.

That night, I type out a letter on my computer. It is awkward and doesn't fully explain what I feel. If I could narrate the letter for Locust, I could maybe make the meaning clear. What I want to say is simply, "I love you. I love who you are, exactly as you are."

But the letter says this:

Dear One,

I'm sorry if my questions yesterday hurt your feelings or made you feel as if I didn't support you. I love you so much. My job as your mom is to support you, love you, and encourage you. Sometimes, though, my job is also to ask you hard questions, to make sure you've thought things through.

You DO think things through, but to be a good parent, I still need to ask those questions.

I love that you are getting stronger every day and more secure in who you are. I love who you are. You said this morning that I shouldn't call you by Locust because it's just easier for me to call you Scarlett. Here's the thing though. You shouldn't have to wait for me, for you to be who you are.

Change is hard. It's not always comfortable. I think of a caterpillar becoming a butterfly. While the transformation is quiet, it's also radical. Imagine the shifts that happen beneath the surface. In this way you are changing too, and it may take people a while to catch up to the internal changes you've made.

I am bound to make mistakes through this. But I hope you can give me a little support too, as my kiddo, to know that I am your biggest fan, your biggest support. I might be awkward sometimes and say the wrong things, but give me a little time and I will make changes too.

I love you, Locust. I will think of you this way in my mind along with they/them. When you are ready for me to call you by your real name, the name that reflects who you are, just tell me.

I'm so glad you've started talking to me about this. What an honor to have your trust! You have my trust too.

Love you!

-Mom

***

I slip the letter under their door.

The next day, Locust comes downstairs for breakfast. They heat up veggie sausage, and I hand them a croissant. "You want some fruit salad?" I ask. Locust nods.

When I hand them the small bowl of fruit, they take it from me and then reach for my hand.

Three squeezes. Our silent code for saying I love you.

I squeeze back.

***

I call Ryan to talk to him about what's happening with my daughter, who is, I guess, my kiddo instead of daughter. I don't want to text it. Ryan is with his family for a couple of weeks. They've rented a big house by the lake. He's slipped away to talk to me, and I can hear laughter in the background. I so wish I was there with him with kids in the water, picnic stuff laid out, music playing, the scents of coconut oil and grilling burgers in the air.

"It's hard, what you're going through," he whispers. "But you'll get through it. Our kids are who they are, and we just love them. That's our job."

He says goodbye after a minute or two, and I am soothed. He took time out to call me and I think about what he said: that your job as a parent is just to love.

***

I start to call them Locust.

I slip sometimes and use the old name, the name that feels like home to me, but it is a name that is home for me, and not for my kiddo. I feel mournful some days, but it's a mourning I can live with. Our children are never fully ours, are they? Not if we've parented them right. They are supposed to change. They are supposed to become a person beyond our expectations.

Locust asks if they can get a haircut, and I schedule it. Off come the long tresses, and when I pick Locust up from the salon, there is this new person standing before me, smiling wide, glowing from the inside out. Their hair is short, masculine. I can see the shape of their face now in a way that wasn't evident before. The curve of their neck. There is such strength in my kiddo, and I don't know how I never really noticed. All this time, this version of my kiddo was hiding and now here they are.

Here they are.

We go to Goodwill. They buy trousers and shirts from the men's department, but also skirts and floral sweaters from the women's area. As I push the cart around following my kiddo, I notice how silly it is to have clothes separated by gender. They're just clothes. Why is something with flowers only meant for women? Why is a suit jacket only for a man?

Locust tries on different outfits and they're laughing, having fun shopping. They've always hated looking for clothes and I realize now it was because they felt they were shopping for a body that didn't belong to them.

So I'm standing in line to pay for the clothes and I feel teary. I realize that all this time, for years, Locust has been struggling to be someone they weren't. They were struggling to be a version of themselves they thought would make everyone happy. They made us happy for years, and now they've realized the person they need to please is themselves.

We aren't so different, Locust and me. They've just had the realization of self long before I did. I am so grateful. Watching my kiddo feel delight, feel comfortable, is an unexpected gift.

In the line to check out, the clothes piled in a heap in front of us, Locust squeezes my hand three times. I squeeze their hand back about twenty times. I love you. I love you. I love you. And then I squeeze their hand three more times just to be sure until Locust says, "I get it, Mom."

# 38. Ryan

It takes me by surprise, but I think I've fallen in love with Ryan.

It actually does feel like falling, but it also feels like sliding, the easy way you step into a warm bath and it feels so good. Loving him is familiar.

We talk every day, usually by text, sometimes on the phone. We see each other here and there: breakfast, coffee, a quick walk together while mosquitos swarm around us.

But we don't have many nights together. His schedule is busy. He has his boys more than half the time and he is not ready yet to introduce me to them. Of course not, we've only been dating for a few months. He's met my kids, but my kids are older. His kids are still young enough that if they met me, there'd be confusion as to my role. Dad's girlfriend? A potential stepmother? It's an awkward dance, but I'm okay with it. All of this takes time. A relationship takes time.

I know I need to check my heart, keep it in balance, be realistic in my expectations, but there is something about Ryan, and there is something about me when I am with him. It's a gentleness. An ease. A sense of belonging. I've been married twice and had countless boyfriends, but I have never felt this comfort before.

It scares him, I think.

"I'm not entirely sure I'm ready yet," he says.

We're sitting on his front porch in the Adirondack chairs. I've brought over Chinese food. His is shrimp and veggies, mine is tofu and veggies. The birdsong is clear around us.

"Ready for what?" I ask.

He just looks at me.

"I'm not asking for anything," I say. "Am I? I mean, I haven't asked or mentioned anything, right?"

"No, but..."

He doesn't have to say it. We both understand. There is a feeling between us and it makes me think of the future, commitment, adventures together, and love for years and years and years. I can't hide that I feel this way. I don't want to. Feeling feels good.

"I know. I'm not asking for anything," I say. But then I have asked, haven't I? Not all at once, but every time we see each other, there's another ask. They don't feel like asks to me. They feel like ideas, like opportunities to spend time together, build a deeper connection, create memories. I say, "Let's go kayaking! Let's go for a weekend up north! Want to go to New York with me? Can you get together this weekend? There's a new restaurant I want to try."

I ask and ask and ask, delighted by the adventures we could have together, if he would just try. In my mind, I can see everything unfurling before me, and it is so good and so easy.

So I ask.

But he has trips planned. Work. A weekend with his book club buddies. A golf vacation with his boss. He has packed his summer schedule. He says he filled it before we met, and he guesses maybe he's been running a bit, filling up all his free time. There is no free time for me yet. There are never any free weekends, or kayak trips, and when he goes up north, it's with his boys, who do not know I exist.

But I am okay. I breathe through it. He just needs more time. He just needs a little time, I tell myself. We are adults and moving slowly. This is healthy, right? This slowness?

Erin says, "Bullshit. He's not treating you well. He's treating you like a fucking Tuesday Girl. Don't you see it? When's the last Friday you had together? When's the last date?"

There have been no Fridays. No dates. "He's not ready yet," I say.

"Honey, you know what that means, right? When he says he's not ready yet, he means he's not ready now. And he's maybe not ready ever."

It is a pain that pierces. It's something I don't understand. When love finds you against impossible odds, when you find a connection and comfort that is unlike anything you've ever experienced, why wouldn't you want that?

Why wouldn't he want me?

I tell Erin thanks, but she's wrong. I'm not a Tuesday Girl to him. I'm a Forever Girl. He's just not ready for forever...yet.

# 39. Phone Calls

My mom calls three times in a single week and I don't want to answer the phone. I ignore the calls, but she keeps calling and part of me wonders if there is an emergency. Is someone sick? Has someone died?

I'm just starting to feel strong again, like I have the emotional strength I lost over the last years with Matthew. Things aren't as raw anymore. I can get through the days without crying or struggling or being frustrated. But a single call from my mother triggers me. What does she want? What does she need from me?

On the fourth call, I answer. "Hi, Mom."

"Hi, honey! We haven't talked in so long! I'm just calling to check in on you."

"Okay. I'm doing okay. How are things with you?"

"I'm doing great! I haven't felt this good in a long time. And Frank is just wonderful. He's the best man and we are just so happy. You know I stay at his place most of the time now, and we're going to move in together officially and he's just wonderful."

"That's good to hear."

"Have you met Frank?"

"I have," I say. "A couple of times. He seems nice."

"He's the best man and we are just so happy. Can we come see you? I haven't seen you or the kids or Matthew in forever. Why is that? Why don't you want to see me?"

There is so much I want to say. I want to say the simple truth, which is so cold it burns. I want to say I don't want to see you. Because when I see you, I think of all the years you weren't a parent to me. I think of the neglect and the hurt, of the times you left me alone while you dated man after man after man. I think of the thunderstorm in the middle of the dark night that was so bad, trees crashed outside. I was eight or nine and I crawled under the bed for safety, and I screamed for you. I screamed *Mom! Mom! Mom!* over and over until my throat was raw and you never came. You never came because you weren't in the house. You were out with some boyfriend who was so wonderful and who would take care of you and change our lives. It feels like my throat still hurts in screaming for my want of you. I think back over the years and how you needed so much from me, and I gave it, but I am spent now. I think of the last time you saw me and Matthew and the kids. You went on and on about how wonderful Matthew was and how lucky I was to find a man who would take care of me and Matthew was so handsome and I was so lucky. So lucky! And then you told the kids a story about your best friend and how she died by walking into an empty elevator shaft, falling to the ground, and her body was mangled so badly they couldn't recognize her. My kids were terrified and I didn't know the story was going there and didn't think to stop you from talking, because you just talk and talk and talk and meander and wind and loop. I was honestly zoning out on you while I cut fruit for a salad, and by the time I noticed the kids' expressions it was too late and the damage was done. I think about how you are a person who needs, not just simply to be in the room with someone else, you need to be listened to, responded to, coddled, encouraged, lifted up, praised. Your need is a thousand open hands crying *gimme, gimme* and I just can't. I can't. I don't want to. I don't want to anymore because the connection a daughter should feel for her mother, is not a connection I have with you. If I squeezed your hand three times you would ask me what was that about? And you wouldn't even listen to my answer. You'd just keep talking about Frank, how happy you are, how great life is, and maybe would I have a few hundred dollars to help with the rent coming up.

Why haven't I invited you over in so long?

Because I don't want you here. I don't want you here in my kitchen, in my house, in my heart.

But I can't say that, so I say something else. "Mom, there's been a pandemic. You live in a retirement community. We can't visit right now. It hasn't been safe. It's not personal, it's just how things are right now. We all need vaccines first."

I tell her Matthew and I have been divorced for a year but he is doing fine. He seems happy. The kids are good. Things here are fine.

It isn't that I lie to her but there is so much she doesn't know about my life, that it doesn't even feel worth mentioning.

"Well, I'm doing great," she says. "The best I've felt in years. Frank is just so wonderful..."

We say our goodbyes and then hang up.

An hour later she calls again and leaves a message, wondering why I haven't talked to her in so long, and why I haven't invited her and Frank over to see me and Matthew and the kids.

# 40. The Truth

Erin is not herself, but that's to be expected. Her house is empty and she's in the situation I was a year ago. In an empty home that feels more empty, not only because of the space left behind by your partner, but because the future you had planned in that space is also gone. All the tomorrows that were before you are *poof*. Gone.

When we walk, the energy we had before is different. Erin is angry. And hurt. I try to understand. Our situations though are so different. When my marriage ended with Matthew, it ended because I asked for it to be over. I insisted. She never wanted to be here. She never wanted to be on her own.

I talk about Ryan, and when I talk about him, I can feel the glow warming inside me and spilling out.

"So you had coffee this week?" Erin asks.

"We did!"

"And how long was that?"

"How long?" I'm confused. "Well, less than an hour, I guess. He had a meeting with a client in India. On Zoom, obviously. He didn't fly over there."

"And when are you going to see him again?"

My glow begins to cool. "I don't know. We didn't make a plan."

"But it's not going to be this weekend, is it? Or next? He makes plans with everyone else in his life, but you just conveniently fit into the spaces. I mean, how fucking long have you been dating now? Four months? And you're still giddy over a half hour coffee? When is he going to take you out? When are you going to have a weekend together like you keep asking? When is he going to make you a priority?"

I don't answer because she is hurting me. It's like she's kicking me. I don't understand her cruelty. I don't even say that out loud, but she can read my silence.

"Goddammit. I'm not trying to be mean to you! It's just, you are at the beginning of this. This is the time when they can't get enough of you, when every moment is about when you can see each other next, and when can you kiss and fuck, and when can you steal away to be together? Four months in and you still don't know the next time you're going to see him."

"You're being really mean, Erin."

"No, I'm not. I'm being honest. I'm being truthful. Because goddammit I wish someone had been truthful to me. I wish twenty years ago when I was besotted with my ex, someone had pointed out the red flags to me, the ones I willfully ignored. He never wanted to spend time with me, and it never changed. I had to fight to prove I was good enough. It never gets better than those first few months. Those first few months are the best it will ever be. When they're courting you is the best behavior you can hope for, because after that, after they're comfortable with you and years and years have passed, they won't fucking try so hard. And Ryan isn't even trying at all with you. If you think somehow magically, he's going to fall in love with you and have all this time and space for you, you need to wake up to the truth. The truth is he doesn't want you, and unless you realize this now, you've got a load of hurt waiting for you in the future."

We finish the walk but I don't say much. I know she's talking about her relationship right now, but what hurts me the most is that there really is truth in what she says. He doesn't want to spend time with me. He doesn't make plans. He doesn't want to introduce me to his friends or family. He fits me into the spaces between meetings or time spent with others. And we never do all the things I ask to do. There are no kayaks. Or weekends away. Or dinners where I dress up and he takes one look at me and says, "Wow."

And I want the Wow. I deserve the Wow.

It's a pain I don't want to acknowledge and I really fucking hate Erin for making me look it square in the face.

I'm in a relationship mostly of my own invention. Ryan doesn't want me, not really. And the tomorrows I have created with him are largely fantasy.

I'm not part of a couple. I'm single.

I love him and he doesn't love me back.

It is completely humiliating.

# 41. Texts

ME: Do you think you could make some time in your schedule for a weekend with me?
RYAN:I would love that. When? I have a trip to LA next weekend, and then I have the boys. The following weekend, I have to help my boss with remodeling his kitchen.
ME: What about the next weekend after that?
RYAN: In a month? That seems like a long time.
ME: I mean it is a long time, but if that's the next hole in your schedule, then that's the next hole. Can you save that for me?
RYAN:...
RYAN:...
RYAN:...
RYAN:Okay.

***

Something doesn't feel right, and that night, I put the Bumble dating app on my phone. I don't want to do this, but he doesn't have time for me. I want a relationship that's real. I want love in my life, and isn't that possible? Or is that asking for too much? Maybe what I have with Ryan is the best I can expect. Is Erin right, that this isn't how it's supposed to be? That there's something better?

I think about what I want in my life. It's not that I want to be married again, but I do want companionship. I want someone to laugh with, have sex with, go on fun trips with. I want someone to text and talk to and curl up on the couch with. I want to make dinner with them. I want deep kisses. I want to call him when the kids are over and just chat and say, "I can't wait to see you again." Of all the things I want, Ryan only gives me one. He texts me.

After he said okay to the weekend plans in a month, he didn't offer any ideas. Will we go somewhere? Maybe up north? I get excited thinking about the possibilities, and then I try to ground myself.

I post my pictures on the app and set my intentions. "Passionate and successful, looking for an eventual monogamous relationship where we laugh and have adventures together. I'm fairly fit and would love it if you were too. Fans of charcuterie a bonus."

I choose pictures where I look warm and inviting and try to find one that shows off enough of my body so they know what to expect. I'm not petite or thin. I'm very curvy, a size fourteen. If they're looking for an athlete, they'll need to keep searching.

Every picture I post, and every prompt I answer hurts me. I don't want to do this. I have a monogamous relationship, don't I? We're exclusive. We are only seeing each other and yet much of his time is spent with others. Still, I have the man in my life I want. I just don't have enough of him.

While I'm contemplating, a cute man likes my photo, so I like him back. What the fuck, right? He texts me on the app:

> KEVIN:Hey! You're an audiobook narrator. So epic! People say I have a great voice. How did you get into the biz?
> ME: Uhm. Are you reaching out because you want to date me or for career advice?
> KEVIN:Ha! You're a little too old and not really my type. Could we meet for coffee and talk shop maybe?

I immediately delete the app. My heart pounds. I don't want to do this. The connection I feel for Ryan is so real and so strong and so fucking right. Maybe Erin just doesn't get it. He's a single dad with two kids. He had a bad breakup. He just needs, maybe, a little more time.

***

> ERIN: I'm sorry.
> ME: No worries. It's fine.
> ERIN: When a woman says it's fine, it's never fine.
> ME: It really is. It's all fine. We're good. I know you just care about me.
> ERIN: I do. And I want someone worthy of you.
> ME: He's worthy. We scheduled a weekend away!
> ERIN: ...
> ERIN: ...
> ERIN: Okay. Good. When? Where?
> ME: Still working out the details. It'll be in a month. He's super busy.
> ERIN: A MONTH?
> ME: We're working out the details. I'm happy! A real weekend!

ERIN: Okay. Walk tomorrow?
ME: Yes. Of course.

***

ME: What do you want to do on our weekend together?
RYAN:Weekend?
ME: Uhm. We talked about this yesterday. In a month?
RYAN:Right. So sorry. I can't do the full weekend.
ME: ...
ME: ...
ME: But you said
RYAN:I misunderstood. I can do Saturday. I'll come up with something great. I'll plan it. Okay?
ME: So all day Saturday? Going away overnight?
ME: I'm not pressuring you; I just need to know so I can get someone to watch my dogs.
RYAN:My son has a game in the morning. I can pick you up after that so maybe 1p.m.?
ME: Oh. Okay.
RYAN:We'll do something great.
ME: Okay.
RYAN:Okay. Good. Great. We can work out the details soon.

***

I realize later, he never confirmed if we were spending the night together.

The weeks pass. Erin and I walk. I narrate a few romance audiobooks. In every book, there is passion and connection, and ultimately, the heroine gets what she wants—a land where she lives happily ever after. I want to be like her, but I'm afraid my voice betrays that I'm starting to doubt it's possible.

***

RYAN: So sorry. Game running late. Be there soon.
ME: When? I'm sort of just waiting here. And you never told me where we're going.
RYAN: So sorry. One more hour and we'll be together.

***

He picks me up at three instead of one. I'm wearing a nice dress, and he's wearing a pair of shorts and an old T-shirt.

"I thought we were going on a date?"

"We are! It'll be great!"

"But I'm overdressed."

"You look fine. But, yeah, maybe you want to change?"

I head upstairs and put on yoga pants and a T-shirt. Before we leave, I write a note for the dog sitter. I've got my overnight bag and Ryan notices and looks at me sadly.

"But I thought..."

"I know. It's just really hectic and my ex refused to take the boys tonight so..."

I call the dog sitter, leave my bag, try not to cry.

***

He takes me out for soup. It's a restaurant about forty minutes away. It's too early for dinner and I'm not really hungry. "The best clam chowder in Michigan, I'm telling you," he says.

It's sweet, I guess. He knows I like clam chowder. But this is not what I had in mind for our weekend together. Everything is tilted sideways.

I taste the soup. It's average. On the watery side.

After the soup, we walk outside by the water. It's pretty and I think it would be a romantic spot to take a picture. When I pull out my phone, he steps away and points to a sign he wants to show me. I put the phone away.

We watch the water, and then he takes me by the hand and says, "Let's go."

I am home by 6:00 p.m.

> ERIN: Hope your amazing weekend is amazing! Wear that bra you bought. Your boobs will bring him to his knees.

I am too embarrassed to text her back. I don't know what is happening. I don't know how I got here. I don't understand that the only place I want to be right now is with Ryan, and not snuggled on the couch with my dogs. I don't understand how the weekend I thought I'd have with him turned into a three-hour excursion for watery soup.

# 42.THERAPY

I start seeing a therapist because I'm confused. My heart, my head, everything is jumbled. We meet online because Covid is still out there, and the idea of talking in person is scarier than the actual talking.

"Tell me what brought you to me," she says.

"I mean, I'm doing pretty great really. Right now, at least. I haven't been doing too great until now."

"Tell me more."

I take a deep breath because I really don't want to go into it. I just want to get a few answers to my confusion, and then get out, but I can't get those answers unless I set the stage. I'm so tired of setting the stage. I want my background to drift away from me. I want it to be an island I'm no longer connected to and have it just sink into the ocean as I move closer to the mainland, but I can't seem to get away from it. I'm tied to it somehow, dragging it along.

"I'm dating someone and I'm really confused. Like he's sending me a lot of mixed messages and I want to know, I can't tell anymore, if I'm hysterical or overanalyzing what's happening. I mean, everyone's a little fucked up, yeah? Starting over is hard, starting over in your late forties is impossible. We're all a little bruised. Bent. Broken. Aren't we?"

"I can see that. Can you tell me a little bit about growing up? Where you've been and where you're at?"

"Honestly, I've been in therapy most of my life and I feel like I've recovered from my childhood. I can talk about it freely now, and it's not because I'm numb and don't feel anything, but it's because I've talked it into the ground. I've done the work, the healing, all the things."

"That's great. I'm glad to hear you've done the work. Can you maybe give me the highlights?"

I take another deep breath. And I tell her. I just put it out there. "So, I had an abusive childhood. My mom neglected me. It doesn't sound like a big deal, but it was. She was looking for a husband from the time I was five until I left to live with my dad when I was thirteen. Mostly, with my mom, I remember being alone. I'd wake up in the morning, go to school, come home from school, make a snack, she'd come home and get ready for a date, pop a TV dinner in for me and then be gone. I was alone. All the time. And my brother wasn't around either. He was with his friends.

"And then I moved to my dad's. And it was bad. My stepmom was abusive. She was diagnosed as multiple personalities, but I guess the diagnosis now is dissociative disorder or something. I feared for my life some days. And some days were great. I'd know as soon as I walked into the room. I could read her body language, and based on that, I knew how to act, what to do, how to talk. You couldn't have emotions in my house, because if you did and she reacted, you could get hurt. My dad didn't do anything to keep us safe. He told us we knew what triggered her and it was our job to make sure we didn't trigger her.

"I had responsibilities toward her. My stepsister and I were on suicide watch, to make sure she didn't kill herself. That was a lot of pressure for a fourteen-year-old. I got used to it, but I told myself I'd never put myself through that again.

"So, I stopped feeling. For a long time. And when I left that house, I made a vow to myself. I promised myself if I ever had kids, I would protect them. I would never put my love for a partner over the safety and love for my children. And I also vowed I would be up front about my feelings. If I felt something, you'd know it. So, therapy, blah, blah, blah. I've done it. I'm healed."

I wait.

"Okay," she says. She adjusts her glasses. There is silence. Finally, she says, "I'm glad to hear you've done the work. And now you're dating?"

I nod. My throat hurts a little. "Starting over again. Divorce number two. In my first marriage, we didn't really know each other. We wanted kids. I moved home after 9/11 from New York, met him, we got married, and had kids. But you could've lifted me out of that relationship and put another woman in my place, and he wouldn't have noticed. We broke up.

"I married again. I loved him. For a long time. And then his depression took over and his condition made me and my kids walk on eggshells. When he started having suicidal ideation, I kicked him out."

There is more to it than that, of course, but I hope this is enough for her to go on. After a bit, she nods. Adjust her glasses. Talks to me.

"You've been through a lot of trauma. First with your childhood, but also later with experiencing 9/11. I imagine that was a really tough experience, going through those things. You've had two kids and two divorces. But you've kept some promises to yourself. You put the safety of your kids first, and you kept your promise to not hide what you're feeling."

I start to cry then. She gets it. She sees.

"Yes!"

"And now?"

"Now, I'm dating and I'm confused."

"Why?"

"Because there's something...niggling at me. I mean, this man, he's not like anyone I've met before. When he looks at me, I instantly calm. He feels like home to me. But there are times when he seems connected with me, and other times when he's..." I hold out my palms. "It's like attachment theory, yeah? Like I'm anxious and he's avoidant. But the potential I have with him, how I can see our future, it's incredible. Home feels really good and I'm not sure why he's pulling back. I don't understand why he doesn't want what feels so good. Unless I'm imagining it? Maybe it's just all in my head. This is what I mean! I'm lost. I'm really lost. So, I need some help."

She thinks for a moment. I'm not sure what I expect exactly, but it's not what she says. "He feels like home to you? And you see potential?"

"Yes. Yes! So much." I start to breathe a little easier.

She nods. "I've been a therapist for a while and I'm going to say something to you I've learned with my other clients. With your history of abuse and abandonment, a man who feels like home to you is a red flag. Bigger than a red flag. This is a dangerous man. If he feels so familiar to you it's because something in you recognizes and responds to the dysfunction. You know the rules here. You know how to react and what to do, and it's going to end up hurting you. Badly. And if you see potential with him, that is also a red flag.

Potential is fantasy. Potential isn't real life. I encourage you to really look at what is, and not what could be."

I want to punch her. I want my money back. What a spiteful thing to say. I don't get to feel love? If I feel love, it's a red flag? Fuck you. Just fuck you!

I don't say anything.

She gives me some suggestions of books to read and says she's happy to see me again if I want to.

I look at her with an expression I'm sure she can read, even over a computer screen.

I'm never seeing you again, you cold bitch.

The anger surprises me. I don't like it. I don't like it one bit.

I sign off, close my computer, and try not to think about the meeting with her.

And I think of the meeting over and over, especially when I see Ryan again.

# 43. LUKE

My kids are old enough that they keep to themselves mostly. I try to give them space. I have a fifty-fifty parenting plan with their dad. One week at my house; one week at his. It's been this way from the beginning. I wonder, sometimes, if I had pushed for full custody, if I had asked for child support and alimony, would things have been different? Would things have been easier for me? But then I think of my own dad and how he checked out, and how my whole childhood I yearned for a dad, and I know I did the right thing. I didn't fight with the kids' dad. I insisted and agreed to fifty-fifty parenting, because I wanted him in their lives. I just didn't want him in mine.

Most of that is true.

But there is also the truth when we were splitting up, and I mentioned having full custody, their dad said he'd never let that happen. He'd fight me in court. I'd been a stay-at-home mom and he controlled all the money, so how could I fight? What would I fight with? I had a couple of hundred dollars of my own. It wasn't until I got a few gigs as a narrator and intercepted the checks when they came in the mail to set up my own bank account, that I started to have any real say in how things would go.

So the narrative now is tweaked a little: I pushed for fifty-fifty, but the truth is I accepted that because I was terrified of losing my kids entirely. It angers me, sometimes, the power men have, especially when you take care of the kids. They have the money and power. You are seen as siphoning from them.

It was okay. The struggle was okay. He has come around and is a good dad to them. Still, though. Still.

We keep this parenting plan for ten years, and then I start to see fissures in the routine.

I'm surprised when I start to realize the kids don't seem to want to go to their dad's house. The Fridays when they switch to his house used to be an easy thing, and now there's tension. My son snips at me. He asks if he can go on Saturday instead of Friday. My other kiddo's anxiety spikes. They stop over more for clothes, books, to ask me a question, to grab a snack.

I feel guilty because I have grown accustomed to the downtime. A week off to live the life of not a mother, but a woman.

But I am a mother. All the time.

Then Luke tells me in a burst, in a flood, what I was starting to suspect, and it comes out in a wave of words.

"I can't do this anymore!" he says. He's sitting at the kitchen counter, running his hands through his hair. His hair is crazy looking, and his voice is high and tight when he speaks. "Every fucking week I have to go to a different house. Pick up everything. Move everything. My clothes. My computer. My Xbox. Every fucking thing. And the houses are so fucking different. Different rules. Different food. At Dad's house there are so many people, and here it's just you and I have my own space, but there, it's like nothing is permanent. I had a shelf in my room and my stepmom decided she wanted it so they took all my stuff off the shelf, put it on the bed, and took the fucking shelf! I don't even have a space that is mine. I'm exhausted. I'm losing my mind. And it's not fucking fair. Don't interrupt. Don't tell me all the reasons I have to switch to Dad's. I know all the fucking reasons and the thing is, they don't matter. You guys make me feel like I don't matter and I fucking do. I fucking matter! I want one house. One space. One thing that is fucking mine. And it's killing me inside that I don't have a good relationship with you or dad. You don't have a fucking clue. Every day is the same drill over and over and I'm floating all the time and I just want to be settled. I just want to be anchored, you know? All this fucking floating around and you know what? I'm not doing it anymore. I'm not. I'm not changing houses. I'm staying here. I can't fucking take it anymore. Don't tell me to go back to the schedule. I don't want to do it. For once, maybe you could listen to what I want instead of making all the choices for me."

He seems to run out of breath.

I take a breath for him.

I'm his mom. I'll probably always do that. But he's right about the choices. It's time he started making some on his own, the way that I've been doing over these last couple of years. I've been starting over, and my son is just plain *starting.*

I am heartbroken to hear this from him. And he doesn't know. He doesn't know why I left his dad or how, in the marriage, I also felt like I was floating. And controlled. And that I didn't matter. So I get everything he's saying. I do. I am proud of him for advocating for himself.

But this will change everything. How do I have time to myself? How do I see Ryan? How do I have more than work and mothering if all I have is work and mothering?

It's a ridiculous question. You don't get to be selfish when you're a mom, and I have been selfish. I have taken a shelf from my son's room without asking. And he wants the shelf back.

"Let's talk to your dad," I say. "And go unpack your things. You're not going anywhere."

"I'm not?"

"No," I say.

He looks at me and smiles and then laughs a little, like he can't quite believe it. "Okay," he says. "Okay."

# 44. Bistro Bella Vita

ME: Do you think we could go out? Like on a date?
RYAN:Of course. I'm not sure when though. Tricky schedule.
ME: Right, but do you think we could get something on the schedule?
Like in a week?
RYAN:Next week I have the boys.
ME: Okay, so the week after?
RYAN:...
RYAN:I'm sure we can work something out.
ME: I just need some time with you. You're losing me, you know?
Could we just have a nice night out? If it's the money, I'll cover the cost. Maybe in two weeks?
RYAN:I could do Wednesday maybe.
ME: But what about Friday? Could you do it next Friday?
RYAN:...
RYAN:...
RYAN:It sounds like this is important to you. I'll make it work.

***

I am so excited for our upcoming dinner that I don't even give myself time to feel embarrassed about having to pin him down to spend time with me. I have this fantasy of the love I want and what I want in my life, and I know that if he'd only bend a little, try a little, he'd feel it too.

We'll go to my favorite restaurant in Grand Rapids. A place that's big and open so it'll feel safe. Covid restrictions are lifting, but small spaces still feel scary.

Bistro is a terrific restaurant. Just a little trendy, not too trendy. They have great cocktails. Homemade pizza. Good desserts. It'll be on the weekend and I'll wear my green and white flowered dress. And heels! I'll wear a fucking pair of heels. Because we'll be out together on a date and I want to celebrate that.

All of it feels forced, but I ignore it.

On the night of, he tells me he's running a little late but he should be there in time. I wait in my living room, pacing a little, teetering in my heels. I check my makeup, my false eyelashes. The dress is tight and shows my curves. I look happy. I feel nervous.

When the dogs bark at the door, I take a deep breath and open it. He looks me up and down and says, "Wow."

If I had written this scene, that's the line of dialogue I'd have given him. This is the line of dialogue every woman wants to hear when she dresses up for her man. And then I notice what he's wearing. A pair of khaki pants that look a little dirty, an old gray shirt. The shirt is a button-up shirt, but it looks wrinkled. "I should've stopped at home and changed first," he says. "I'm sorry. I was helping my boss at his house with some renovations and I just didn't think."

"It's okay!" I say, my voice high pitched. "You're here. You're here! And we're going to have a great time."

It feels good. It feels like a date. It is a date, isn't it? Except I'm dressed up and he's not. I'll pick up the check, because he can't or won't. But I have my date night. I have it.

***

We order the burrata cheese plate as an appetizer. I order a martini. Ryan takes a sip. "I don't want to drink too much," he says and smiles. Drinking, he says, makes it hard for him to orgasm, so I know what he's referencing. I wasn't sure if he was going to spend the night, and I am so happy.

So I drink a martini. He has a sip or two.

We laugh over our appetizer. Groan a little with how good it is. He reaches for my hands and we hold hands across the table. "I feel like I've been letting you down," he says.

My eyes get teary and I don't want them to. My eyelashes will float right off my face if I let them. "It's okay," I say. It's hard to talk. It shouldn't be this hard to talk to him. It scares me for some reason, the idea I might say the wrong thing and he'll just disappear from my life. I'm terrified to lose him. "You're here now. It's just, it's been hard. You're so busy. And sometimes I feel like..." I can't say it.

He squeezes my hand, gets me to look him in the eyes, and holds my look. It calms me. It always calms me when he does that. I say, "You don't have time for me. You don't seem to want to have time for me, and I'm confused. Do you want me to see other people? Other men?"

"I mean, I'm not a jealous person, really, so if that's what you want to do, I understand."

It's not the answer I expected or wanted from him. "You wouldn't mind if I saw other men?" It doesn't register. Does he not care? The thought of him seeing other women devastates me.

I try to pull my hands away but he squeezes harder. He looks me in the eyes and he is teary. "Listen to me," he says. "I don't want you to see other people. I don't want to see other people. I just want to see you, and I just want you to see me. Okay?"

"Just me?" I ask.

"Just. You."

I smile then and the tension I feel, the disappointment at his dirty pants, his lateness, how I'll pick up the check, all of it fades. He is here with me. He hasn't said he loves me, but he only wants to see me, and this is where it starts, doesn't it? This is how relationships evolve and change and deepen.

I order the mushroom entree and he orders a pasta. We split a dessert and I have another cocktail. I am warm and floaty and I can't wait to get home and have him unwrap me from this dress.

He does unwrap me. He kisses me all over. And when we make love, we look into each other's eyes, and I can feel strands of ribbon swirling around us and tying us together.

I orgasm and feel it down to my toes. He doesn't orgasm. "I'm not sure why," he says.

"That's okay," I say and laugh. "I feel great!"

"It's not your fault. It's probably all in my head."

"Okay. I wasn't thinking it was my fault, exactly. It's okay. It happens sometimes."

I try not to think of when my Matt couldn't finish and it was because he wasn't attracted to me. Matt and Ryan are not the same person. And Ryan is attracted to me.

We cuddle in bed for a bit and just as I'm about to drift off Ryan asks me if I'll walk him to the door.

"But I thought you were staying over," I say.

"I can't tonight. I have an early run with my group tomorrow."

It's only nine o'clock, but I get it. I wrap myself in my silk robe and walk him to the door. He pulls me close and kisses me again, but it doesn't feel quite right. Things look right. The dinner, the way he said we should only see each other, but everything is slightly off. It's like looking at a reflection in the mirror and your mirror image moves just a breath before you do.

"I'll see you soon," he says. "Lock the door, okay?"

I nod. I wait until he closes the door behind him before I lock it.

I should feel happy and sated with good food and drink and time with my boyfriend, but mostly, I just feel worn out.

# 45.The Thing About Heartbreak

The thing about heartbreak is you can feel it coming. You can see the glass on the side of the counter, just balancing, and you know that any wayward wind is going to push that glass to the ground and it will shatter. You see it. It's inevitable. You know it's going to happen, but you just hope it won't happen yet.

And then the wind comes.

I make it through the end of summer with Ryan. He promises if I just hang on until the end of summer, he will have time for me. "I'm so sorry. We met in April and by that time, I'd already had my summer scheduled. But once we're through with August, I'm open."

"And you'll add me to the schedule?" I ask, eyes wide with hope.

"I will add you to the schedule." He smiles. I smile back. He kisses me and squeezes my hand. And I want to believe him.

A week later, I get a text.

RYAN: Great news! I'm going to be in *The Nerd*! The local theater contacted me and I'm going to be in the show. They really need me to fill in for someone."
ME: But what about your schedule? What about us?
RYAN:I'm so sorry. There will be plenty of time for us. I asked them. I still have my weekends available until a couple of weeks before the performance.

Only he doesn't. He gets Covid and has to recover, and then the weekends are spent with his boys, and they add in rehearsals to make up for all the time they've lost. I have even less time with him. I have no time with him. Just his morning texts, an occasional emoji.

When he comes over, it's just to have sex, and the last few times he couldn't finish. "Don't worry," he said, "It's not you. I'm sure it's not you. I'm just tired. I have a lot on my plate." When he says "It's not you" it feels like he's saying *"It's you. I'm not really attracted to you anymore. You can't make me orgasm, because you're not pretty enough and your wanting of me is a weight."*

I've been working on being honest and authentic, and instead of carrying these thoughts around, I ask him.

ME: Have things changed? Are you losing interest?
RYAN: Nothing's changed. Just really busy. Still feeling crummy from Covid.

Another week passes and there are no coffees, or cooking together. No movies, no weekends, no time. I spend my time alone while he is busy with theater, friends, family, and a life I have no part of. And I can't wait anymore. This isn't working.

"Fucking *tell him*," Erin says. So I do.

ME: You are losing me.
RYAN: Just hang in there. I can't help all these changes.
ME: Should I start seeing someone new? Someone who has time for me?
RYAN:I have time for you. Just hang in there.

He says I can come see the play, but not on opening night. He is too nervous for that. I get it. I perform audiobooks for national companies. I've gotten awards for those performances. He's starring in a tiny local show. He's a little embarrassed. "I don't want you to make fun of it," he says.

"Of course not. I know it's not a Broadway show. I'll adjust my expectations accordingly. It's a group of local people coming together for live theater. It'll be wonderful. When do you want me to come?"

He can't decide. He says he'll let me know.

The week the show opens we decide I'll see it on closing night and then I'll spend the night with him. It will be our first overnight together in months. But later in the week he says that closing night won't work after all and wouldn't Friday be better for me?

Friday is not better for me.

And I watch that glass on the counter and the wind blows and everything changes. It happens that fast. Because now even though my head knew, my heart knows it now.

I am in love with Ryan and he does not love me back.

There is nothing that will change that.

I can be my best self, my sweetest most loving self, I can be passionate and excited, I can be understanding and supportive, and I will always only be someone he fits into the spaces of his life. There is nothing I can do to prove I am good enough. I am good enough. He just doesn't want me.

I try to envision seeing him the night before closing. How will he acknowledge me? Will he introduce me to the cast as his girlfriend? Will he kiss me? Hug me? Shake my hand? We've been exclusive for over six months and I still don't know how he thinks of me. I feel like a secret. I feel like he's ashamed of me.

I need someone who is proud to be with me. I need someone who will brag about me.

I text him. I'd tell him in person but I just don't know when I'll see him again. He's going away for the following weekend after the show with his sister and brother. So I text him.

> ME: I am not going to the show. I'm not going to see you again.
> I wait for the dots to show, but they don't, not for hours.
> And then, later that night...
> RYAN: Well, that sucks. I think I'm maybe not as ready as I thought. I just can't be anyone's person yet.

You're never really ready to be someone's person, though, are you? But you try anyway. You try even though you're scared and being vulnerable is actually painful. You try because what is possible is so amazing, you are willing to risk it. You try because in losing the person, in living your life without them, your life is grayer and cold.

But he doesn't mind losing me.

Because he never loved me to begin with.

When Erin calls me, I can't even speak. Finally, I say, "Shattered." And she knows what I'm saying.

She saw the glass balanced on the counter too.

She saw it on the very first day.

# 46. I Know What I Want

I move on. I move on because that is what you do. My relationship with Ryan wasn't healthy, and I need to just get over it. I try not to think about him or all the things I thought we were going to have, the relationship, the travel, the joy. Those were just fantasies.

I focus on myself, on tiny things that bring me joy: my paint-b- number kits, my walks with Erin. I take a class on mushroom foraging and join a hiking group. I watch scary movies, write my blog, and record audiobooks. I start mentoring. I fill up the spaces of my life with tasks. I guess, maybe, I start running away from things a bit, the way that Ryan did. I fill all the empty moments in my life with tasks and appointments and goals.

I know what I want, and it is simple. I want someone to spend time with. Someone who I don't need to convince I am worth knowing and loving. I want shopping trips to Costco, a night out at a restaurant. I want to learn how to kayak with someone, to forage for mushrooms with someone, to watch movies and share popcorn. I want sex and connection. I want to fall asleep with someone who is my equal, my partner, and then wake up with him grateful to be next to each other.

It doesn't feel like it's asking too much, but everything in my life says it's asking too much.

"What's a healthy relationship?" I ask Erin. We're on her back porch and she's just had me carry an Adirondack chair that is, I imagine, actually heavier than a linebacker. I'm sweating a little.

"What do you mean? Don't you know?"

"I mean, I think I do. It's..." I take a deep breath, and not just from the chair. "I think it's when someone likes you, wants you, respects you. But is that a thing? Have I narrated romance novels too long and now I'm looking for the impossible?"

We sit down. A hummingbird zooms over my head. "Fucking hummingbirds," Erin says. "Every time you're here or I talk to you on the phone, they zoom on by. I tried to take a picture of them for an hour yesterday and they never showed up, and you show up and here they are!"

"My spirit animal," I say.

"Something like that. I know people who have good relationships, I think. I had a good relationship for years, until I didn't. And it was easy. We loved spending time together. Sex was good. I could go to him with my problems, he could come to me with his. It was a bit of a dance really, only neither one of us knew who was leading. My parents have been married forever. And don't your aunt and uncle have a healthy relationship?"

I nod. "They do. I'm just wondering if their relationship is the rule or an anomaly. I'm wondering if I want too much. Maybe I should have been okay with the little that Ryan could give me."

"Oh, for fuck's sake. He gave you nothing. There's something wrong with that dude."

"I know. But maybe what was wrong with him...was me?"

Erin's face is tight and I can tell she's trying really hard, but then she laughs anyway. "Honey, fuck. No. No, it's not you. It's him. He couldn't make time for you. He filled his life with a million things and none of those things involved you. That wasn't healthy."

"But it felt real. It felt like we could've had something great."

"That's the fantasy, right there. That's your hormones or whatever. Didn't your therapist say to beware of the man who feels like home to you?"

"That's hardly fair," I said.

Erin nods again. "I think we go wrong with thinking that life is fair. It's like those survival shows you keep telling me about, right? You have this survivalist who's dropped off in fucking Alaska and they can make their own clothes, forage their own food, create weapons from a pair of sticks, and what takes them out? A fucking splinter that gets infected. The world isn't fair. The world is a fucking beast."

"It feels like it could maybe be a little bit fair."

"Maybe."

"I'm going to try the apps again."

"You should."

"I don't want to."

"But you should."

"You should too," I tell her. Her face reddens immediately.

"I'm not ready. Fuck that shit. No. Nope. Not yet. Not ever probably. I'm just going to live in my nice house and die alone."

"Is that what you want?"

"It's what I want right now. Things were good for a long time, and things could still be good if he'd wanted them to be, but he changed all the rules. He sent me a text from New York. He got a commercial. Can you fucking believe it? A fucking national commercial. He's living his best life. And here I am."

"At least you've got hummingbirds," I say. "And me."

"That's healthy," she says. "I think." We're quiet for a bit. The leaves rustle. Another hummingbird zooms by. "Okay," she says. "Let's go shopping. Show me the app. You talking to anyone yet?"

I take out my phone, pull up the dating app, and sit next to her. "I'm talking to a few men," I say. "But they're not Ryan."

"No, they're not. And that's a good thing. Remember that."

I nod and pull up the first profile.

# 47 Recovery

The man and I are walking the Reed's Lake loop that Erin and I usually walk, but much more slowly. I said I didn't feel comfortable meeting him at the restaurant for a meal, but we could meet outside the restaurant and take a little walk. "Sure," he said on a Facebook message. "Walking is great! I walked six miles yesterday. Thank you so much for meeting me. Again, I'm really sorry I stood you up all those months ago, but I promise there was a really good reason for it."

I'd like to think there was a good reason for it, instead of him just being cruel. It was humiliating, sitting in the restaurant, waiting for him to show. I don't mind going out alone, but it was the humiliation in getting dressed up and looking forward to a date, and then having to sit there just waiting.

All those months ago, he'd contacted me on Facebook after reading one of my blogs. "I don't know if you remember me from high school. I mostly hung out with your brother, but I remember you. We're both single and...would you like to have dinner with me? We can catch up?"

At the time it seemed delightful, meeting someone I sorta knew three decades ago. I agreed. We texted. He wanted to take me out. We set a time and place. And then he never showed, and never wrote.

I'm not sure why I agree to meeting him and risk being stood up again. Maybe it's because you hear strange love stories all the time. I've narrated a lot of them. *They went to school together and never knew each other and BAM, they met and fell in love.* I don't really think that's going to happen, but it's someone who wants to spend time with me who is not Ryan. I need to keep meeting people. I thought Ryan was the One, and I was so wrong. So maybe there is another One. I won't know until I try.

Is my heart fluttering at meeting this guy? No. Mostly, I just want to hear why he stood me up. He'd said it was a good reason. Maybe he was sick, so I am thinking he has cancer probably. That would be terrible. Maybe he had Covid and didn't want to tell me. There's a shame that accompanies being sick, which is silly, but it's true.

He wants to explain it to me and apologize, and I don't know, maybe fall in love?

When I see him waiting for me in front of the restaurant, I already know there won't be any love. I feel guilty for making that quick of a decision, but sometimes you just know. Maybe it's pheromones, or maybe it's just my soul reaching out and saying, "No. Not this one."

He is so different than Ryan, but it's still Ryan I want. Maybe, then, there's just no room in my heart for love.

We walk.

I adjust my pace, slow down. I wore my workout clothes, but this is going to be a stroll. He's limping and seems out of breath. Of course, I tell myself, the dude is dying of cancer. Give him a break. "You want to sit?" I ask.

"We can walk. I've already done 15,000 steps today."

I try to believe him. There's a sheen of sweat on his forehead. He's wearing sunglasses, and I can't see his eyes.

We sit.

Then he starts talking. He doesn't ask me any questions. There's no small talk, it's just him and me on a bench, the warm air around us, space between us, and I just listen. That's what he needs me to do and maybe I can offer this small kindness.

"Yeah, so, I got sick the night we were supposed to meet. You probably guessed that. See, so, okay, I'll just say it, I'm an addict. I have been for years, I guess. They've told me I shouldn't live on my own, but I was managing, doing just fine really, but the night I was supposed to take you out, I kind of went over the top at work. I'm an attorney and I guess it started in school. Or maybe it started in high school. I'm, you probably noticed, short and maybe it was to get girls' attention or something, I don't know. But I started pretty early with drinking and then drugs. It was cocaine in college. Then it carried over into work. You've got to be energized or, you know, hopped up, to take out clients, go golfing, go to clubs, and it was fun, it was *really* fun. It was really fun for a long time, and maybe I've just done it a little too long, maybe. On the night I was supposed to see you I took a little too much or there was something in it, they lace it with stuff now, and I ended up, well, I ended up getting real sick. Then because it happened at work, I got called on it, and I agreed to go to rehab and that's where I've been the last six months.

So I wanted to tell you how sorry I am, but also tell you that I read your posts and you're alone and I'm alone and that's really hard, isn't it? To be alone? And we don't have to be. I thought we could maybe be together, you and me. I'm six months sober and I have a review at work next week and they'll probably slap my wrists, but it's a good job, a stable one, and I have a car, and a place to live. I have a nice house. Right now, I don't sleep there. I sleep at another place, a sober house, and they tell me that's what's best for me right now, to have that support, you know? And I'll have to take medicine for the rest of my life, but it's okay. I'm okay with it all. Would you like a mint? I had pizza just before coming here and my mom told me I should have a mint because I told her I was meeting you, and she said I'd better take a mint and then she handed me a handful and here. Take one."

I take the mint.

There's a lot that happens in my brain. It's firing very quickly and there are a lot of different things I could say. First, I'm connecting the dots. He got really sick. He overdosed. He has to take medicine for life. The only medicine I know you have to take for life is methadone, and that means that the drug he was on wasn't cocaine but heroin. He lives in a halfway house. He has a review at his job where they're probably going to fire him.

But here is this man, in pain, and lonely, asking me to be with him, to be his partner. He doesn't even know me, but that doesn't matter. Part of it is absurd, the audacity to think that I'd want to be in a relationship with a recovering addict, the sheer gall of him asking me, expecting me to say yes—but also, there's a deeper emotion here. This man is so close to the edge, and I have a responsibility to him. It's not one I want or really appreciate, but it's a responsibility of kindness. I can see he is afraid. I could crush him with a few words, and I don't want to do that. I speak slowly. Give it the weight it deserves.

"I really appreciate hearing your story," I say. "But I think that maybe you aren't quite ready for what I'm looking for. You're so fresh in your recovery, that maybe you need another six months or so. And I need some more time to heal too. So maybe in another six months, check back in with me. Do your work. I'll do mine. And we'll see."

He takes a deep breath. He takes off his sunglasses. His eyes are dull blue. “Can we walk by the water?” he asks.

I agree.

We talk a bit more about science fiction books, mostly, and then I tell him I have to get home.

“Okay,” he says. “Okay.”

I drive home and I don’t know whether to laugh or cry. It’s absurd, really, but it’s also heartbreaking. I hope he makes it. I hope the world doesn’t crush him.

I hope the same for myself.

# 48. Dating

I go on a number of dates. Erin says it's good. "It's a numbers game. Eventually you're going to meet someone who lights you up. You'll meet someone to share your life with."

I am not convinced, but I keep trying.

The men are nice. Kind. Some are attractive. Some are smart. The problem is, every man I meet isn't Ryan.

I meet a sweet teacher. When he smiles, his eyes disappear in the crinkles in his face. He's kind and soft-spoken. He's also petite. I feel like if there was a massive puddle, I could lift him into my arms, trudge through the mud, and set him down safely on the other side. He's half the size of me, but he's cute, and I like our first date.

On our second date, he takes me out for ax-throwing. I'm so terrible that it's painful. We're there for an hour and I keep trying and trying and smiling and trying and failing, every time. I'm smiling and laughing, but mostly, I just want to go home. I remember being with Ryan where my awkwardness was met by his, and how good that felt.

The petite man and I go for a walk with each other, but after that, he stops texting. He's just not into me. I can't blame him. I'm not into him either.

I meet a sculptor who is also a refrigerator repairman. He has strong hands. He orders three gin and tonics while we're out. I'm attracted to him, so I try to overlook the drinking. I'm trying to overlook a lot, just to have companionship. Being lonely is so hard. I tell myself, he's probably nervous. I want to impress him, and so I start to talk. And talk and talk. I don't ask him any questions; I just barrel on and on and on. "What do you mean you're not a sculptor? That it's just a hobby? You have art in galleries. They sell it! That means you're a sculptor. You should own that. I'm also a mentor and encourage freelance people to grow their businesses and there's a few steps you could do already."

He tells me he isn't interested in steps. He likes his job and he likes his hobby of sculpting on the side.

I then outline all the things he could do. Build a website! Sell your stuff on Etsy! Post TikTok videos while you make your art!

I tell him about heartbreak and how in love I was with Ryan, how I probably still am, but it's okay, I'm working through it.

I want to know if he can fix my refrigerator. I'll pay him, ha ha, of course, but it's been broken for weeks and it would be so cool to have an actual sculptor fix my appliance. That sounds like a euphemism, doesn't it, *fix my appliance*, but I don't mean it that way, unless he's interested. Is he interested?

He is not.

He pays for our drinks and when I text him to say thank you and what a good time I had, he asks me not to text him anymore, and I realize that I've become an awful date. I will now be an embarrassing story he'll tell about the woman who, in five minutes, tried to micromanage his entire life.

I'm so embarrassed about it, I don't even want to tell Erin.

A few days later, I meet a really nice guy, but I feel no chemistry with him. We have crab cakes and wine and we laugh and talk about Belize, Ireland, and Scotland. He says he'll take me if I want to go and I actually believe him, but I'm exhausted at the end of the date. I just want...Ryan. I want comfort. I want to go for walks, and make risotto, and I want to text at five in the morning, when I'm up and ready for the day to begin. Most people are still sleeping then. I want someone who aligns with who I am. Honestly, I don't want to be dating at all. Not really. I want to be a couple. I want Ryan back.

Erin says, "How was it?" She's asking about the date and what we ate and was there chemistry.

I say, "It was fun!" You can hear the exclamation point in my voice.

"Fuck," she says. "Fun, huh?"

"I'm just not interested." And what I mean is, "He just isn't Ryan."

Months pass. I narrate. A lot. I hang out with my kids. I hang out with Erin. It gets cold. Christmas comes and goes. I think about what my Christmas would've been with Ryan if I had been more patient. If I'd allowed love to grow slowly instead of pushing it to bloom. I can imagine us waking up together at five, when the world is dark and cold. Having coffee together. I imagine the first gift exchange. At this point, would our kids have met? Would I make a big dinner for us all? Stuffed pork loin, pull-apart bread, roasted green beans with smoked almonds, a chocolate yule log for dessert.

Instead, it's another Christmas alone. I'm texting a musician and we've had a heavy flirtation. He wants to meet, but he's not interested in a relationship. He just wants to fuck. Why not? What am I waiting for? Something with real emotion? A real relationship? I want too much.

He won't be in my area until spring so he asks if we can Zoom on Christmas Eve. When he says Zoom, I know what he means. He wants us to meet online, get naked. It seems ridiculous and not at all sexy, but I agree. It's something, and this way, I'm not technically alone on Christmas Eve while my kids are with their dad.

Our time to meet comes and goes and I text him. "Sorry. Can't make it. Mom in ER. She has Covid."

I start to laugh then, drinking my third glass of wine, in my silk robe and my sexy underwear. Of course, this is how things are. There's no mood killer like a loved one in the ER for Covid.

I tell him to keep me posted, but he doesn't. In fact, he doesn't text anymore. I'm not sure if he was even telling me the truth.

None of this is fun. I hate every minute of it.

In February, I'm sitting in a parking lot about to meet a guy for drinks in a hotel. I've told him I'm not going to his room with him, and it will just be drinks, and he texts, *Ha Ha. Of course!*

I reach for my door handle about to get out of my car and the text chimes. "Canceling," he writes. "Currently puking."

So I sit in my car in front of the hotel, where it is dark, and cold out, and the guy I was supposed to meet is currently puking *while* texting. I'm sort of impressed by that, must be coordinated, but I also realize, he probably found someone to meet who wanted more than drinks. And honestly, I don't even want drinks. I don't want anything with this guy, or any other guy.

I want Ryan.

Didn't we have something good? Why did I push so hard? Did I fuck things up by wanting too much too soon? We weren't together much, but when we were, I felt so at home. So alive! And it wasn't a trauma response, it wasn't, because Ryan was such a kind man. Such a good man. And I don't want to meet these guys. These sculptors, or architects, businessmen or pot growers. I want the guy who giggles and watches *Laurence Welk*. I want the guy who has a full life with his sons, and spends time with his family and friends. I want that. I want a healthy relationship that will, in time, grow to me being a priority in his life. I want his awkward kisses and lovemaking, where things aren't great, but they'll get better with practice. I want him.

So I take a deep breath and reach for my phone. Part of me says, "Don't do this. Move on. You two are done." But the other part of me, the narrator part of me, knows I am writing my own story, and my story is a romance where after some strife, the girl gets the guy, because it turns out he's just been waiting for her all this time.

I text him:

I am sitting in a parking lot and the guy I'm supposed to meet is puking. To be honest, I don't want to meet him at all. I just want to meet you.

I decide to be brave. It doesn't take much to be brave, just a single second. I hit send. The three dots immediately appear.

Would you like to get coffee sometime?

I feel relief in every atom. This nightmare of trying to meet someone else is over. I know what is going to happen because I can feel it, I can feel it and see it. What is going to happen is Ryan and I are going to work this shit out. Ryan and I are going to write a love story.

I text:

How about tomorrow?

# 49. COFFEE.

It's 6:30 a.m. when we meet. Even the baristas are tired. But this was the time that worked for Ryan. It's before the day starts and all his meetings and things he has to do with his kids. I get there a little early, thinking I'll grab a table, sit down, get my nerves under control. But when I open the door, there he is, standing in his orange puffy jacket, looking at his phone.

"Hi," I say softly. "Oh! Hi!"

He looks up and his smile lights up his blue eyes. He looks a little different. He's lost some weight. He looks tired. I am tired too. It will be okay now, I know it.

"Hi, you," he says and then he opens his arms to me and I step in, hugging him. He hasn't slipped his phone into his pocket so the hug is a little awkward, but isn't that just like him?

I pull back. I had all these things I wanted to say, but not a single thing comes to mind. "What do we do now?" I ask. I'm asking about do we sit, grab a coffee to-go, but I'm also asking is this okay, are we going to date again, is this nightmare of meeting new people over?

"Maybe we get some coffee?" he asks. I nod because this is a sensible place to start.

We get our coffees and sit down.

There is small talk, but I struggle with it. I've always hated small talk. It feels like such a waste of space and energy. We talk about our kids, our jobs. The weather. The holidays. He thought of me, he said, on Christmas. I tell him I thought of him too. I don't tell him about the abandoned Zoom call. And then I just can't take it anymore. "Are you seeing anyone?" I ask.

He looks at me. It's important to describe this. He doesn't just look at me, but his eyes seem to connect with me somehow. It's soothing. "I've been dating, but I haven't connected with anyone special," he says. I exhale. No one special. Okay. He could be in a relationship, but he's not. I'm not either. "I waited a while before, you know, dating anyone. I just wasn't ready to, you know?"

I think he's talking about dating, but I'm not sure. He could be talking about sleeping with someone. I haven't seen him in six month and while I've had a lot of dates, I haven't kissed or been intimate with anyone. I just didn't want to.

"I'm not seeing anyone special either," I say, and then the smile that comes to my face is so natural. It's a smile of relief, and hope. This could work. This could be a thing, but one of us is going to have to be brave. "I miss you," I say.

His eyes are teary. He reaches for my hands and squeezes them. His hands are cold. "I miss you too," he says.

"Do you think we could, I don't know, maybe try again?"

He gives me a half smile, but doesn't answer. "Or if that's too scary," I continue, could we maybe start texting again, like we used to? Just try that out?"

"I miss texting you," he says.

"Same," I say.

When we're done with our coffees, he walks with me outdoors and then hugs me. Then he looks at me one last time, connects with me, and kisses me softly. It's not a passionate kiss, but it's not a goodbye kiss either. It's a hello.

The next morning at 6:01, he texts me:

Hello, darling. Did you think I would text?

I answer:

I had a funny feeling you would.

# 50. The Thing About Hope...

I've just filled my life coach in about all the things I've been doing. The walking. The working. The podcast listening. The dating. She knows I'm still recovering from heartbreak. That sounds dramatic, but there's truth there too. So I fill her in on all the things, but I've saved the best for last.

"What's that smile about?" she asks.

"Well, I reached out to Ryan." My whole body is smiling. Ryan and I have been texting and we're planning on getting together on Sunday. He's got his boys, but he'll swing by for a bit. I tell her this. I'm afraid she'll judge me. Say, *he didn't have time for you before. Why do you think anything has changed?*

"Awesome!" she says. "And how are you feeling about all this?"

It should be an easy question, but it's not. Suddenly all the joy I was feeling in telling her the story of reconnecting with him is sucked out. I imagine the vacuum that happens in space if you open a hatch. I feel like there's no oxygen. I can't breathe.

"Okay," she says. "You're okay. Can you tell me what's happening? Your face just got really red and I can tell you're struggling."

I nod. That's all I can do is nod.

What exactly is happening to me? Why this reaction? I'm happy about what's happening with me and Ryan. I have a second chance. We have a second chance. Then why am I sitting in my life coach's comfortable and essential-oiled office having a panic attack.

The awareness hits me at once. "It hurts."

"What hurts?" Her voice is soft.

I point to my heart. "Hope," I say.

"Tell me more," she says.

"Things don't go right for me," I say. "I mean my career is good, and my kids are doing better. Those things are okay. But love doesn't go right for me. I want this so badly, but I'm terrified."

"What are you terrified of?"

"Of it not working. Of being hurt again. But I'm also terrified of it working. How do I do that? How do I love someone again? How do I believe that I can be loved again? How do I get there?"

She listens. Takes a moment to think about it. "What if..." she says and looks at me. "What if good things are possible? What if love is possible for you? What if all you have to do is ask for it?"

"Ask for what?"

"Whatever you want! You've asked for that in your career. You get work. You have enough gigs. You've asked for that in your friendships, your relationship with your kids. What if you allowed for the possibility of good things to happen to you in your love life?"

"You mean ask Ryan to give me what I want?"

"What if you did?"

"But what if he says no?"

"But what if he says yes?"

I can't process this. I never considered, really, I could have what I want. And maybe he doesn't really know what I want.

Maybe I'm making decisions for him.

I start to breathe again. It's okay. Hoping is okay. Hope doesn't have to hurt. Maybe good things are possible. Maybe they are.

***

Ryan and I are chatting while I'm on the treadmill. It's February and cold and terrible outside. I'm so hungry for the sun, for fresh air, for travel. I haven't traveled in over two years.

"I have cabin fever so bad," I text him. I don't expect him to answer. It usually takes him a while, but the three dots appear almost immediately. It surprises me and my smile is wide.

"I do too," he says.

"I've been thinking about a last-minute trip somewhere."

"Where would you go?"

"I asked my narrator friends and they're suggesting Palm Springs in California. I'd have people to visit, things to do."

"Palm Springs is terrific," he texts. "Perfect weather. And they have the nicest airport I've ever been to."

"Well, if the airport is good...then how can I resist?"

"I have serious cabin fever too. My boss said I could visit him at his condo in Florida if I wanted. He has a time share and all I'd need was to pay for the flight."

"When are you thinking of going?"

"A couple of weeks. Not much beyond the thinking stage, really, but I'll check some flights."

I stop the treadmill and catch my breath. There it is. The opening to ask for what I want. I could ask him to go with me to Palm Springs. I could ask. He could say no. He probably will say no and I'll be embarrassed. But what if? What if he said yes.

"You could go to Palm Springs with me!"

The three dots appear instantly. I hold my breath.

"I'd love to," he texts. "Let me take a closer look at things. Can I let you know for sure in a few days?"

It's like some kind of wicked magic. I asked for what I wanted, and this time, this time, he didn't give me an excuse, or a delay or anything. He said he'd love to. HE'D LOVE TO.

Hope, in my chest, is a tender butterfly that's just unfurled its wings in preparation for flight.

# 51. The Joy of Sex

"Did you know you can use your big toe for sex? According to this book, we could go to a restaurant and you could pleasure me under the table with your big toe and no one would ever know."

"Hmmmm. Sounds fun," he texts back.

I've been texting him updates as I read the *JOY OF SEX*. I remember pulling it from the bookshelf in my mom's living room and flipping through the pages, astonished by what these two people were doing and how much hair they had. It was the seventies version of the book. The updated version has a lot more grooming, and it's not quite as titillating.

"We could meet," I text.

"Yes. When?"

I'm nervous when I text him the answer. "What about this weekend?" I'm worried I'm still a Tuesday Girl to him and nothing has changed. But this feels different. How I talk to him is different, how he responds is different. We might be going to Palm Springs together. We're flirting. We're laughing. It feels like we're rebuilding.

"This weekend would be great," he texts back.

And again, I can't breathe.

We go back and forth, but eventually settle on Sunday. He's got his kids this weekend, but on Sunday he can get away. My kids will be at their dad's so he can come over. He'll let me know when. We'll spend the afternoon together. It will be fulfilling, he says.

I'm happy with this. It's not a Saturday, or a full weekend, but this is progress.

When Sunday rolls around, he texts and apologizes. He's running late, but he's still coming. "I can't wait to see you," he says. "Bring your big toe," I say back.

It's not until four when he arrives. I think we'll rip each other's clothes off and make mad love on my living room floor, but he asks for a Mountain Dew and then we chat for a while first. It's been so long since I've felt his skin, and I'm confused. Why doesn't he want me? Why are we talking about grocery shopping? I haven't been with anyone in over six months, since dating him last, and I feel ready to explode. I don't know how many women he's dated, or how many he's slept with, and the realization saddens me. He hadn't met anyone special, but that doesn't mean he didn't sleep with someone. I haven't slept with anyone but him this entire year. I couldn't. But maybe he could. Maybe he did.

When he finally kisses me, it feels a little lazy. A little tired. It's good though. Familiar. Sweet. He says he was with someone, but she was tested and so everything is okay. I don't admit I haven't slept with anyone since him, so instead I say, "Same."

When we finally take our clothes off, I sigh a little looking at him: his tattoos that seem so at odds with his nerdiness, his skinny legs, the slight belly. It's not passion I feel, but comfort.

His phone goes off a number of times while we're together, but he ignores it. It doesn't take him long to finish, and I'm trying not to be disappointed. There's just something missing from all of this, and I hope it isn't my heart. There's a shine he used to have that I'm not seeing or feeling anymore, and I'm not sure where the shine went.

"Do you need to check your phone?" I ask. It's buzzing repeatedly.

"Yeah. I probably should. I told the boys I'd be back in a half hour."

"Oh. I thought...You said we were going to spend the afternoon together."

"I'm sorry about that. You know how it is." He looks at his texts and begins scrolling. "Mr. Dad, Mr. Dad, Mr. Dad." he says.

"Your son calls you Mr. Dad?"

"Cute, right? He's panicking. I've got to go."

He doesn't apologize, but I guess he shouldn't have to. When your kid needs you, you go. Although...why didn't he answer the texts a minute ago? Probably because he was too focused on his orgasm, and now he's not.

I think, maybe, it's cute that his son calls him Mr. Dad, but there's also something distant about it. There's something off about it.

"Did you decide about Palm Springs?" I ask. I'm still naked while he's pulling his pants on and quickly lacing up his shoes.

"Oh, yeah. I'm going to Florida!"

Again, no apology. He sounds happy. "Oh," I say.

I'm embarrassed.

I'm embarrassed I asked, embarrassed I'd hoped. I don't know exactly what I'm doing.

"The flight was really cheap and I have a free place to stay, and it's my boss so..."

"No, I get it," I say. And I do. He'd rather spend the weekend with his boss in Florida eating sandwiches and watching football than with me in Palm Springs, drinking cocktails and making love and being in the sun. I'm trying to write this love story, but the characters just aren't cooperating.

He kisses me goodbye. "I'll see you soon," he says, and then he's gone.

# 52. Winter Wonderland

Erin refuses to walk with me. Not because she's breaking up with me as a friend, but because it's too damned cold. "Look," she says, "I know I was born and raised in Michigan but I'm Sicilian by blood. And we don't go out when it's below sixty-two degrees."

"Erin," I say. "It's below sixty-two degrees seventy-five-percent of the time here."

"I know. This is why I don't like to leave my house. You walk. I'll talk from the comfort of my cozy living room."

So I bundle up. Coat, boots, scarf, hat, goggles, windbreaker, moon boots, ski poles, a polar vortex silver blanket for heat and signaling aliens. I may have overdone it a smidge. I start my walk. It's a blizzard outside, but it doesn't matter. I'm Scandinavian.

"How are things with Ryan?" She puts a little pep in her voice, but I know she's suspect.

"Well, unfortunately, he can't go to Palm Springs..." I stop her before she can interrupt. "But he wanted to. He was actively trying. I don't know, things feel different. It's better. We're, maybe, building something."

"Okay," she says, still suspect.

"I can't explain it. All those dates I was on are supposed to be fun, but they didn't feel fun. Being with him feels fun. Easy. And he's trying. He saw me yesterday."

"Sunday?"

"Yes!"

"On a Sunday?"

"Yes!"

"Okay."

I slip on some ice. I'm not entirely sure what I'm doing out here. "It's fucking cold, Erin," I say.

"I KNOW. THAT IS WHY I AM INSIDE MY HOUSE."

I decide to turn around. I've learned recently if something is terrible, I don't have to suffer through it. Walks. Weather. Bad movies. Marriages.

"Tell me you're still going to Palm Springs," she says.

"Oh, I'm going. I haven't been anywhere in three years. Last time I was anywhere was when we went to New York for the Audies."

The Audies are the audiobook awards, the Oscars of the industry. A book I produced was nominated as Best Original Work. We had three tables filled with our team of narrators and writers and we were drunk and happy. Stephen King was there and his son and some influencers who were supposed to make the event more timely, but mostly they just looked out of place.

"I miss New York," Erin says.

"I miss it too. I miss everything."

"But you'll go to Palm Springs."

"Alone."

"That's okay. You'll have a trip in your future."

"I so want that," I say. "You know I never traveled with husband number one. We were too busy with babies. Husband number two and I went a couple of places. But you know when you travel with someone you love, what's the first thing you do when you get in the hotel room?"

"You have sex," Erin says.

"Yes. Only with Matthew we never did. We'd take a nap first. Travel is tiring."

"It's too bad Ryan couldn't swing the Palm Springs trip. You'd have had a lot of sex. And cocktails."

"Guess I'll just have cocktails," I say.

"And sun. Man, think of the sun."

I'm hit by a bitter blast of wind. "I just want to get out of here," I say and I mean everywhere. I want a vacation from life. From all the things I have to do and should do. From all the mess of everything. I want to wear a bikini and be warm and eat cheese and drink too much. I want to come home relaxed and happy and at ease.

It would've been nice if Ryan could've gone with me, but it's okay. We've got future trips together.

I reach my house, open the door, and breathe in warmth. "Next time I tell you I'm walking outside, tell me to smarten up."

"I did tell you that," she says.

"Next time, make me listen."

Erin laughs. "There's only so much I can do. You'll either listen or you won't."

"I'll listen. I promise." I shut the door behind me.

53. Texts

ME: I'm super anxious. I don't know about this trip.
ERIN: You are always anxious before you travel.
ME: I am?
ERIN: Yes. Every time we go to New York, you say this same thing. You just haven't travelled in three years.
ME: Fuck. You're right. I've forgotten how to travel. I've forgotten how to people. What do I pack?
ERIN: Just pack everything.

***

ME: Are you ready for your trip?
RYAN: All set. Really excited for some sun.
ME: Me too. I wish you were going with me.
RYAN: I know. Me too. But I've got a group of seventy-year-old men who want to watch football and eat sandwiches.
ME: Yeah. No contest really. Passionate weekend with me vs. giant sandwiches with old men.
RYAN: Ha! I can't wait to kiss you when you're back.
ME: We'll kiss each other. We'll be sunburned and it will hurt.
RYAN: And that will feel so good.

***

ME: There's so much sun. I don't know what to do.
ERIN: Get out there and enjoy it!

***

ME: First cocktail picture. I don't know what they call it, but it's pink and there's a flambeed grapefruit on it so I'm good.
RYAN: Drink all the cocktails. We are going for a walk.
ME: Your old men friends walk?
RYAN: Some of them do.

***

Instagram posts of crab cakes, pink cocktail, smiling in the sun. Pictures of the place where I'm staying, the pool in the backyard, the desert, and the mountains stretching across the horizon.

***

ERIN: Are you breathing? How is it out there?

ME: Everything is so big and so bright and so wonderful. All I want to do is purr.
ERIN: Good plan. Do that.

***

ME: How was the walk?
RYAN: We saw crocodiles!
(Picture of crocodiles)
ME: On your walk? Were you scared? Did you sacrifice one of your friends so you could escape?
RYAN: Now we're getting Cuban sandwiches.
ME: Oh, Cuban sandwiches in Florida! The best. Can you send me one?
RYAN: I'll get right on that.
ME: There is more sun here than where you are. You send me the sandwich. I'll send you some sun.
ME: I wish you were here with me though.
RYAN: ....
RYAN: ...
RYAN: They only have a really small TV here to watch football.
RYAN: I wish I was with you too.
ME: I think I'm going to pick up a bottle of wine for myself and then drunk text you later.
RYAN: Do it!

***

ME: The only thing b0ow about drunk texting is that autorcorrect fixes most things. Autorcurrect ignores the things you want fixed and rewrites the things you don't want fixed.
RYAN: It's okay. I can still tell you're drunk.
ME: Is because I asked if you want to make out?
RYAN: Maybe. Also the typos.
RYAN: I do want to make out.
ME: I'll be home in five days. You'll be home in two, so you'll have to wait for me.
RYAN: ....
RYAN: ....

***

ME: I am just tecting you to let you iiknow that I havd a bottle of wine. Well, not the whole bottle. And it is 7:30 here which means it's 10:30 there and I AM STILL AWAKE. This is the wonder of travel. I am awake when normally I should be asleep and it is not blizzarding out and I am not in my house that I haven't eft for three years and this is so much fun. Why didn't I travel before this? Oh right. My life was falling aopoart. How is your life?
ERIN: Kinda falling apart too. I'll tell you when you get back. 10:30 is too late for you. Go to bed.
ME: Taoo late. I am alrerady asleep.

***

ME: Sweet dreams, Ryan. Sleep well! Dream of kissing me. I'll dream of kissing you too.
RYAN: ....
RYAN: .....
RYAN:

# 54. Deep Thoughts

The trip is just what I needed. I thought I'd go out to Palm Springs and spend my time alone and in a hotel room, watching murder shows and being depressed, but it hasn't been like that at all. A narrator friend rented his Airbnb to me and we have breakfasts together on his back porch by the pool. We talk about work and life, his time in New York. His struggles. What happened when he came out to his family, and how it affected his career. He tells me of a great love affair in Paris, his heartbreak, and how he eventually found his way to the desert and a career and a home.

I meet a producer's mom for coffee and we talk outside in a garden, surrounded by other people soaking in the sun. She was a teacher and now she's on her final year. Retirement is right there in front of her and she can do all the things she's always wanted to do, but she's not quite sure what that is anymore. She lost the idea of who she wanted to be. She remembers wanting to write poetry but hasn't given it a shot yet. We talk about our love for writing and how words rescued us. She says this next year she'll maybe figure out who she is now.

I meet another friend for Korean BBQ. She and her husband are trying to have a baby, but it hasn't happened. Not yet. "I feel like this is one thing I'm supposed to be able to do, just naturally, you know, and I can't. It's like feeling like a constant failure every time I get my period." They're looking into IVF treatment. I tell her of the friends I've had who've lost babies, who couldn't conceive, and then later, they did. It'll happen. They'll have a family, I know it. She tells me I'm going to be okay too. "Love is going to work out for you." She tells me about her heartbreak and meeting her husband and falling in love when she just didn't believe it was possible anymore.

I meet another narrator at a diner. It's like being on the set of that old '80s show *Miami Vice.* Everything is pastel with neon lettering. She tells me she hasn't had work as a narrator or a director in the last three years, since before the pandemic. "I think they've forgotten about me," she says. "I let them know I'm here and available but I just haven't gotten any gigs. Maybe I'm not assertive enough. Or maybe it's all the Hollywood and Broadway people who have flooded the market. Why would they need me when they can have a superstar instead?" She talks about the trouble she had in her first marriage and how she never felt like he supported her, and now she has a partner who loves her completely as she is.

Finally, I meet another colleague outside of Palm Springs. We find a Mexican restaurant advertising Happy Hour. We order giant size margaritas and a bottomless basket of tortilla chips and salsa. We talk a little bit about narrating, but then talk about our own work. She's got a big book coming out; I'm still trying to find someone who'll take my work on. Someone who believes in me. She tells me about the struggles she's had in life, in love, in career. She's happy now, but it's been a journey. Man, it's been a journey.

We get drunk. We stumble around outside and she shows me a swanky resort made up of little cabins or cabanas or whatever. "Writers used to hang out here. The guy who wrote *It's a Wonderful Life.* Hemingway. Fitzgerald. Imagine those parties here. Imagine all those stories inside all of those rooms. All those people. All those years."

I can hear the glasses clinking. The music in the air. Their laughter and mumbled conversations.

I drink wine or cocktails or coffee. I eat sandwiches or breakfast or salads. I talk and I listen, oh, I listen to these wonderful people. And I start to realize, slowly at first, but then, as it happens, all at once...I realize everyone is struggling. It isn't just me and my few years, or my lifetime of disappointments and letdowns. Everyone has something they're going through.

Walking through the grounds of the resort, I can get glimpses of people inside. Their rooms illuminated. There are families or couples or single travelers. And in those rooms, there is pain and heartbreak. Unbelievable struggle and loss. There is the hope for love or a baby or a job, and there is that cold waiting that happens when you're sure that what you want most will never come.

We are all struggling.

And we are all figuring it out.

On my last day in Palm Springs, I don't have to try and breathe or try and relax. I just do. My skin is sun-kissed and my body soft. I'm going to go home and it will still be cold, and I will still be figuring things out. That's what you do. You feel whatever it is you're going through, and you figure it out. That's called living. And that's what I'm doing.

# 55. NEW YORK

"Tell me everything," Erin says. We're about to be elbow deep in some serious pasta dishes, and we haven't talked in three days. It's all very exciting. We tried talking while I was traveling, but it was hard. Plus, she kept telling me to get off the phone and go soak up some rays.

"You look good," she says.

"I think I gained five pounds. And I'm sunburned."

"Exactly. That's what I said. You look good." She nods toward the artichoke dip and I dive in. Again.

I tell her everything. The trip. The food. The people. The time I spent driving through California mountains, all the lush curves, how different it felt. "It felt alive, and vast. So fucking beautiful. Every now and then I'm reminded that you think you're breathing until you actually get some oxygen, and then you go, oh, this is what it means to breathe. I'm not sure what I've been doing all this time."

"Yeah, it's like suddenly we're discovering we've been breathing nitrogen all this time and not oxygen."

"It's amazing we're still breathing at all." I pass Erin a breadstick.

"And tell me the rest of it," she says. "Did you see Ryan when you got back?"

I nod, smiling. "Yesterday. And a crazy thing happened."

"Okay."

"We were texting and he said he couldn't wait to see me and kiss me and all that nice jazz, only he has his sons and..."

"Ugh."

"No. Wait. So, he said he could meet me for a quick drink before he picks up his boys. And we met. In person."

"He made time to meet with you?"

"He did! It was really quick, but...don't make that face. Let me explain. He said he wanted to ask me in person. He said he felt bad about not going to Palm Springs with me but he had this crazy idea. His favorite musical is playing in New York, *The Music Man*, and he said we should go. We could go as soon as possible, do a whirlwind twenty-four-hour trip. Stay in the city, see the show."

"Holy shit! He asked you on a trip?"

I nod, excited. Beaming from within. “It won’t exactly be Palm Springs, but you know how much I’ve been wanting to go to New York, and to go with the man I’m dating? It’s a dream come true.”

Erin looks impressed. “So maybe things are a little different. He’s never asked you anything like that before. That’s a sex trip if I ever heard of one.”

“I know! And things feel good, you know? I was talking with my life coach and we were discussing trust. She has this exercise where you get two mason jars, and when someone is starting to build trust with you, you put a marble in the jar. Like every time he says something nice, or we make plans, or he follows through, I put a marble in the jar.”

“What if he fucks up? Do you take marbles out?”

“Probably. I didn’t ask about that. The point is, for the last month, every time we talk, I just keep putting marbles in the jar.”

“What happens if you fill it?”

“I don’t know. I win a pony, maybe?”

“Fuck,” she says. Our pasta arrives, and we don’t say anything for a while. We just grunt and moan. It’s actually kind of embarrassing.

“So, when are you going?”

“In two weeks! He called last night and we looked at tickets. He bought the tickets, I reimbursed him, and then I covered the plane fare and will get the hotel room.”

“Why’d you reimburse him for the tickets if you’re getting the flight and the hotel?”

“I have points and his budget is kind of tight. It doesn’t matter. Two weeks!”

“What day?”

I don’t want to tell her.

“Do not fucking tell me it’s Tuesday.”

“But...listen. The tickets are super expensive on the weekend. And Monday is dark on Broadway. Tuesday made sense. In two weeks, I’m taking a romantic whirlwind trip to New York with the man I’m seeing and I’m excited. Can you be excited for me?”

She smiles, but it's not a real smile. I give her a look. "I am excited for you, but for the record, Ryan has not filled *my* marble jar, but this is a start."

I nod. Take one more bite of pasta, then push it away. Erin pushes the dessert menu toward me. Like I even have to look. Crème brûlée.

"And what's been happening with you?" I ask.

"Hmmm. So. Uhm. My ex? He's, uh, back. He loves me and he wants to try counseling again. He just doesn't know if he can do it, if he's good enough for me or whatever, but we're going to try. I'm going to try."

"Fuck! Erin! You should've started this conversation! Way to bury the lead."

"I didn't want to take away any of your California glow. But yeah. So that's happening."

"You don't seem excited. Are you excited? This is what you want, right?"

"I don't know what I want. I thought so, but I just don't know."

I think about it. "Well, you will know. You'll be in your session with him and you'll know if you want to keep working on it, or if you're totally done. And either way you'll have your answer."

"You could say the same thing," she says. "You'll go to New York with Ryan and then you'll have your answer on whether you want to keep seeing him."

"Look at us, about to figure shit out," I say, still smiling.

She orders the brownie sundae and we chat some more but I don't say the thing I'm thinking out loud. I'm just holding on to the thought close to my heart: I already have my answer.

# 56. Summoning the Monster

Over the next couple of days, I organize everything for my overnight trip to New York with Ryan. I upgrade our seats on the flight, and choose a really cute hotel near the theater. I daydream a little about flying out there, first class, we'll start with mimosas, and then I'll show him the city. There's a little bit of New York in my heart still from when I lived there in 2001. A little sparkle that even 9/11 couldn't take away.

I make sure the kids will be at their dad's, and Matthew agrees to take the dogs. I organize my recording schedule so I can take the day off when we get back, because I'm sure the travel and late night will affect my voice, and I don't want to record a romance while sounding like Bea Arthur. (Nothing against Bea Arthur.)

I putter around the house, cooking and picking up a bit, walking the dogs, and I think how Ryan is letting down his guard, and slowly letting me into his life. We will hold hands on the flight, take a taxi ride, check into our hotel and he will kiss me as soon as we check in. There will be no kids or obligations. He won't have to work, and we'll be traveling together. Our focus will be on each other and New York and the musical, and I am so excited I can't even think straight.

So when Erin calls me, I miss the tone of her voice at first.

"Is it too early to be packed and ready to go?" I ask her, giddy.

"You don't leave for another week and a half. So maybe a smidge. Did you decide what you're going to wear?"

"Not exactly, but they're both velvet, both low-cut, and I feel great in both of them. One is long and rust-colored, the other short and green."

She doesn't say anything and that's when I feel it. "You okay?" I ask.

"You got a minute?"

I tell her I do. Of course, I do. I start my coffee and put in my earbuds so I can listen.

"We did two counseling sessions and I guess I have my answer."

"That quick? You know?" I pause. Something's not right. "Are you, uhm, moving forward?"

"Fuck yeah, I'm moving forward. Just not with him."

"Oh, Erin," I say, my heart breaking. My coffee gurgles in the background, but I know I'm just going to sit there and let it get cold.

"Turns out way back when, I was right about everything. Remember when I told you he'd replaced me? Well, he did. First with his coworker Amber and then with his other coworker Emma. Amber and Emma. Sounds like a fucking burlesque show. Probably was."

I don't say anything. I'm not supposed to right now.

"And it's not that he's been fucking around. Fine, I get it. I stopped sleeping with him ages ago, so whatever. Go fuck somebody. But what gets me is he's been lying to me all this time. All the time when I said he'd replaced me and he'd cry and cry and say 'Baby, no, it's not like that. I'm just working extra.' He fucking lied to me. He said he was just focused on other things. He just needed time. He didn't know what was wrong with him, but he hadn't replaced me. Not at all. He looked me in the eyes and said he never did anything or felt anything with those women, and he fucking straight up lied.

"Worse than the lying is the gaslighting. 'I'd never do that to you! What are you saying? Why are you making all this up?' He'd treat me like I was crazy, like I was hysterical, and all along, all these last years, I've been right.

"What makes it even worse is that I made him into a monster. I did it. If only I hadn't demanded intimacy. To be included. If I hadn't wanted to talk about our problems. If I hadn't challenged him on his career choices, on his finances, things would be okay. If only I'd kept my fucking mouth shut and adored him like I did for the first two decades, we'd have been fine. If I'd fucked him more. Worshipped him better."

It hurts me to hear her say this. It hurts because she's probably right. I say, "You know that's not true, what you're saying, right? You didn't make him into a monster. He just couldn't handle a healthy relationship. He wanted the glimmer of your adoration and when that faded..."

"He went and found that glimmer with someone else."

We don't say anything for a bit, then she continues, "He said he still loves me, that I'm the best thing to ever happen to him, that he doesn't deserve me, and maybe he can work on things. I just need to give him a couple of more sessions with the counselor. He doesn't want to lose me. He just needs more time. More time! I've given him two decades and now he wants more? What the fuck do you need more time for? You either want to work on this or you don't. It's an easy decision. But that's the decision, though, isn't it? When he says 'I don't know what to do' what he's really saying is 'I don't want to be the bad guy. I want to fuck new women but I can't break up with you because then I'm not the hero, and I really need to be the hero.' That's the truth. So you know what I said? I pointed right in his face and said, 'You're right. You don't deserve me.' And I grabbed my stuff and left."

I want to cheer for her, but it's not that kind of moment. Because she loves him. With everything in her, she loves him. And he hurt her. He lied to her. He treated her like she was crazy and all the while, she was right about everything. He needs to be the hero and when she stopped worshiping him, he couldn't handle it. I think of Matthew and if only I'd been quiet. If I hadn't pried too much, wanted too much, strived for too much. With men, there's a line you need to walk to keep them happy, and Erin and I haven't been doing it. Somewhere along the way, we just stopped.

"It's terrible, isn't it?" she asks. "The person closest to you in the world can look at you, hold your hands, and tell you things that aren't true."

I'd say I can't imagine it, but I can. It's brutal.

"The worst lie was that he said he loved me. You don't love someone and then replace them. That's not love. That's something twisted." She pauses. "I'm really sorry I took away your joy about your upcoming trip with Ryan. I want to be happy for you and I'm really trying to. It's just hard right now. You're going to look great and it's going to be great, and I promise we can talk more about it and be excited and happy and all that."

"You didn't take any joy away from me. I've still got that. What you're going through is real and it deserves some space, yeah? I love you so much, you know? Just think, six months from now, we're going to look back at all of this and...well, we're not going to laugh because this shit isn't funny, but we are going to be proud of ourselves for being true."

"In six months?" she asks.

"Yep," I say. Convinced.

We hang up.

All night I'm haunted by the thought of how you can know someone for years, and they can still look you in the eyes and lie to you.

# 57. Texts, a Message, and More Texts

ME: Good morning! I woke up thinking about our trip. I'm so excited!
RYAN: I am too. I've always wanted to see a show on Broadway.
ME:I've seen a number of them. You'll love it.
RYAN:Only one week to go!

***

ME:I've decided on the shorter dress for New York. I'll wear the long dress to your Audies party this weekend.
ERIN: Perfect. Audies party is fancier than NYC. I wish we were all in New York for this, but at least you're going next week.
ME:Your party will be awesome. I've already got the menu planned.
ERIN:Is Ryan going to come with you?
ME:I asked him to and you know what? He said Yes!
ERIN: Didn't your life coach tell you to ask and you'll receive or whatever.
Ask for the lotto numbers.

***

ME:You still good with coming to the party this weekend? It's a bunch of narrators and publishers from the local audiobook community. Fun people. I'm not nominated this year, but it'll still be fun, and I'd love to have you on my arm.
RYAN: Yes. Still coming. Will have the boys so I can't stay long, but I'd love to meet all your actor friends. I've always been envious of your narration gig.
ME:You could give it a spin sometime in my booth if you want.
RYAN:Okay! Cool. What time on Friday?
ME: 6 p.m.?

***

ME:Menu: shrimp cocktail and macarons. I'll just pick those up. Charcuterie.

I'll put tons of cool stuff on it. Then, I'll make those brie pastry puffs, chips and dip, and sfeehas. Everyone loves a good meat pie, yeah?
Even vegetarians.
ERIN: You don't mind doing this?
ME: Are you kidding? I love feeding people. I've hardly cooked at all in three years.
This will be a blast. And Ryan is confirmed coming.
ERIN:I picked out my dress. Can you take pictures and we'll look happy and we  can post them so our exes can see how happy we are?
ME: HELL YES. We're going to look amazing!

***

Facebook Message/Instagram message/email:
MARILYN:
I'm sorry to bother you but my boyfriend Ryan just broke up with me last night, and I see you gave him money for tickets a few days ago. Is there something I should know about to protect myself?
You seem really cool and I just want to know.
We went away Valentine's weekend to New Orleans and I found a birthday card from another woman (not you). He said we would work on it and go to counseling. Then randomly broke up with me and now my mind is racing. We've been together for two years. No animosity toward anyone, just broken and looking for answers. I'm so sorry for bothering you.
ME:...
ME:...
ME:...

***

ME: Erin? I'd call but I can't talk. I just got this message and I don't
understand. What is happening? Can you take a look and let me know?
ME: <Sends screenshot>
ERIN:...

ERIN:...
ME:Can you explain what she means?
ERIN:Holy fuck. Go to her Facebook right now. Check her profile.
ME: ...
ME:....
ME:....
ME: Erin, there are all these pictures. Of them together. It's Ryan and her. There are a bunch of pictures. Pictures he sent me on his trips, but they're trips he was on with her. And they were in New Orleans.
There's the alligator picture. But he was in Florida. I don't understand.
What is this? Why the fuck would she contact me? Who is she?
ERIN:Oh, honey. I'm so, so, so sorry. Can you talk?
ME:I don't understand what this is. I'm going to text him.

***

ME:I just got a disturbing note from a woman named Marilyn P. She said you were dating her for two years and you just broke up with her. Can you explain this to me? Is this true? I went on her Facebook and there are all these pictures.
ME: Who is she?
ME: You said you weren't seeing anyone. But the pictures show the ball game you went to the day after we met in April, and she's there with you. And she's at that concert you said you were at with your writing partners. And she's with you in New Orleans when you said you were in Florida and I was in Palm Springs. And she was with you yesterday. Ryan? What is this?
RYAN: ...
RYAN:...
RYAN:...

RYAN: I can explain. I do know her.
ME: Please call me.
RYAN: Give me a few minutes.

***

ME: He says he can explain. He's calling me in a few minutes.
ERIN: What are you going to do?
ME: I'm going to throw up.
ERIN: I'm here. Call me when you're done. With any of it. I'm here.

# 58. The Phone Call

"Hi," he says.

"Uhm. Okay. Hi." It feels good to hear his voice, but I don't want it to. My body is doing funny things. Revving, or something. My voice is even when I talk to him. Calm and soothing. I think I've dropped into my narrator register, which is like my voice, but not my voice at all. It gives me distance. It gives me control.

"How are you doing?" he asks.

"Is that really a question you're asking me?"

"Yeah. Okay." There's a pause here.

"Tell me what's happening. Who is this Marilyn person? And why did she contact me?"

"She's someone...I was dating her."

"Dating her? But she said you've been in a committed relationship for two years. Is that true?"

"No. That's not true. It hasn't been two years. We started dating in April of...Oh. Okay. Almost two years. Well, I guess it's been two years."

"She's been your girlfriend for two years."

"Yes."

"So that's not someone you're just dating. That's a committed relationship."

"Yes. I guess."

"And you just broke up with her last night."

"Yes."

"Last night? When you told me you were with your boys...You were with her. And you were breaking up with her."

"Yes."

"Why?" I'm trying to process this and there's a part of me that thinks maybe he broke it off with her because he's falling in love with me. I feel proud of that. He wants me. But also, that's not rational. Why would I want him knowing this now?

"My brother and sister have been telling me to break up with her for a while now and I finally did it."

"So your brother and sister told you to do it, but you didn't really want to? I'm not criticizing you. I'm sure you can hear it in the tone of my voice. There's no anger here. I'm just trying to understand." There is no sadness or anger or pain or anything in my voice. I have stripped my voice bare.

"Yeah," he says. There's a little energy now to his voice, as if he's excited that I'm understanding. "So remember my brother who passed away? He had this girlfriend, a female friend really, and they were the best friends. They were together for years and years. They were so amazing together, and I always wanted that and I found that with Marilyn. She's my best friend. We do everything together. But the physical part, the attraction I need to have, just isn't there."

"You slept with her though, right? Over those two years."

"I mean, yeah."

"Did you sleep with her last night? Actually, don't answer that. I'm trying to understand. She's your best friend, and your girlfriend, but you're not attracted to her. But you have that attraction for me."

"I do. I do, of course!"

"So when we were dating exclusively, when we met and you knew I wanted a monogamous relationship, you were with her this whole time, but you made me think, you manipulated me into believing it was just you and me. So you could fuck me."

"That's not...what you're saying is really ugly. I never manipulated you."

"No? When you lied about everything? When you told me we were exclusive? When I watched your cat for you while you were on vacation with Marilyn? That's not manipulation? Calling it what it is, isn't ugly. It's just the truth, isn't it?'

"I guess. Yeah. Okay. It's the truth."

"And are you seeing anyone else?" Another pause. Things begin to click into place. "So when you asked me to New York and you said you couldn't go on Saturday, is that because you're with someone else?"

He takes a deep breath and I wonder if it's because he really needs to breathe, or he's thinking of ways to spin this. "Yeah," he finally says. "We're going away for the weekend."

"What's her name?"

"Her name?"

"I'd like to know her name. I know Marilyn's name. And these are women we're talking about, not objects or numbers. So this other woman you're seeing..."

"Jen. Her name is Jen."

"You're seeing her next weekend and you and I are going to New York on Tuesday."

"Yes. We can still go to New York! This doesn't have to change anything, except maybe it's good that you know now. Now you can understand."

"Sure. That makes sense to me. So, you're with Jen next weekend. Are you having sex with her too?"

A short pause and then, "I am."

"Unprotected, exclusive sex with her?"

"I don't want to get into details with you."

"I think I'm owed a few details."

"I always use a condom. She's not on birth control."

What he's saying to me is starting to sink in. My brain is understanding, but it is not connected to my body. What I'm beginning to understand is that everything he has ever told me is a lie.

"And are you seeing anyone else?"

"Right now?"

"Yes, right now. There's Marilyn and Jen and me and who else?"

"Just one other woman. But I haven't slept with her. Yet. I'm pretty sure I'm not going to."

"Ah. Okay."

What else am I supposed to say? All of this is crazy.

"We can still go to New York," he says. "This doesn't have to change anything."

It changes everything.

But.

But...I'm ashamed to admit I want my romantic twenty-four hours with the man I'm seeing in New York. I was promised that. I earned that. I want the first-class tickets, the taxi ride, I want the swanky hotel room, and the frenzied kisses and passionate lovemaking. I want the chaos and the lights of Times Square, and holding hands in the darkened theater. I want Broadway and him to kiss the side of my neck. I want applause, after-show drinks, and slow sex, and an exhausted trip back to the airport. I want to be a character in all the romance books I've narrated. I want things to work out for me. But some stranger, this Marilyn, took that from me because she told me something I didn't want to know. She broke into my life and took away the one thing that was good. She told me the truth. Who gave her that right?

"Marilyn is emailing me. She's telling me about your relationship. I need to know, is she going to hurt me? Is she unhinged?"

"No! No, I promise you. She's not unhinged. She's just sad. I'm sad too. I'll talk to her. I'll tell her to leave you alone."

"Please do."

"Can we still go to New York?"

I think of what I want. I think of all the times in my life I haven't been able to get what I want. I think of all the times people have taken from me: promises, security, love. Maybe this time, I can be a taker.

"We can still go to New York," I say. "But I need a few days. You can't come to the Audies party with me this weekend. I need to make sure...I need to make sure I can handle it."

"Okay. I understand. I'm sorry you found out about this. I really care about you."

"Yeah. Sure. I get that."

"I'll text you tomorrow," he says.

"Okay," I say.

I hang up.

# 59. Party Plans

"What time should I be there tomorrow?" I ask Erin. I've got my checklist before me. I've picked up everything I need for the party, I just need to do some basic cooking and preparing.

"Come over whenever you want. At least by four, maybe? People will start coming over by six. Obviously, Ryan isn't coming, right? Did you cancel your flight and hotel yet?"

"No, I didn't cancel it."

"You should be able to, though, right? With all the Covid stuff, they let you cancel flights now. And you should be able to do the same thing with your hotel room."

"He's not coming to the party. I told him I wasn't sure if I could be around him."

"Of course, you can't be around him. He's a psychopath. And, obviously, you're not going to New York with him."

I don't say anything.

"You're not going to New York with him," she says.

"I'm still going."

Another pause. "You can't go with him to New York, you know that, right?"

"I'm going to go. The only thing that's changed is I know exactly who he is now. There's no fantasy left. But I want to go. I deserve it. I want that romantic twenty-four-hour trip to New York to see a Broadway show with the man I'm dating."

"But...You're not..." Erin exhales. "I don't understand."

I sit in my kitchen at the counter, surrounded by stuff for the party tomorrow. Toothpicks, crackers, cherry tomatoes, bottles of champagne. "I want New York, Erin," I say.

"I get that. And you can have New York. I'll fucking go with you on Tuesday. I don't care how much it costs. Tell me how much and I'll buy my ticket tomorrow."

"He's got the tickets to the show. He won't reimburse me. And he doesn't get to go to New York with someone else. That's my ticket. It's mine." I try to make her understand. "I'm so tired, Erin. I'm tired of not getting what I want. Of having things and people hurt me. I wanted this so badly."

"I know you did."

"But it's more than *The Music Man*. I don't know if I can make you understand. I don't even care about the show. It's not about the show. I want to be loved enough to have someone whisk me away for twenty-four hours and do something ridiculous. I want to be desired enough. I want to feel what that is like. I want that. And some woman I don't even know took that from me."

"She didn't take it from you. Ryan..."

"I know it's not real. I get that. I know that Ryan took it from me. But couldn't she have waited? Couldn't there have been that kindness to let me have something good for a little while, and then take it from me? For once, couldn't I just have something good? I'm exhausted. I'm exhausted by this, but I'm more exhausted by life and constant disappointment. Other people get things. My parents got to act how they wanted. Take what they wanted. My husbands got to make all the decisions and take and take and take. I'm tired. I want this. It's my turn to have something. All I have to do is pretend. I'll smile. I'll kiss him. I'll hold his hand. I'll fuck him in New York. I'll take pictures. I've done a lot of pretending in my life, and I can pretend this one last time. Then when I'm home, I'll say fuck you to him and I'll never see him again."

For once, it seems like Erin is at a loss for words.

"I don't think...It doesn't seem safe. I don't think you're thinking clearly. You don't sound...You don't sound like yourself."

"I'm exactly myself. This is who I am. I'm going to New York on Tuesday, and tomorrow, I'm going to your party. I'll be there at four. The food will be great, we'll look beautiful, and everything will be fine. I can do this. Everything is totally fine."

"Everything is not totally fine."

"But didn't I sound convincing?"

# 60. Naked and True

The next morning, I can't work. I slept terribly. Tossed and turned. I smiled through dinner with the kids and then getting them breakfast in the morning, but my whole body hurts.

Ryan texts me. *Good morning!* he says. *How are you today? Did you sleep okay?* As if this is any other day. As if he hasn't ripped out all the trust and hope from my body.

I think of the jar of marbles and how close it was to full. I see those marbles spread all over the floor around me, rolling in different directions, the mason jar smashed.

Are you excited about your party? What are you making?

I want to throw the phone against the wall, but I just sit at my kitchen counter, calmly drinking coffee. I try to imagine myself on the plane with him, holding his hand, kissing him, him tearing my clothes off in passion and want and need. It makes me nauseous.

> ME: I need to talk to you in person. It doesn't have to be a big thing. But do you think you could come over for a little bit? I need to make sure things are okay.
> RYAN: ...
> RYAN: ...
> RYAN: I can come over. Yes. I'll be there in a half hour.

I wait for him. Finish my coffee. Put it in the dishwasher.

Usually, I'd be excited for him to come over. I'd put on a cute outfit, make sure my makeup looks good. But I don't have the energy for that. I'm so tired. I'm so very tired. My eyes are puffy. My hair a mess. I move in slow motion.

The dogs bark and I know he's at the door. When I open it, he gives me a sad smile. "Hi," he says. I tell him to come in.

"Don't say anything," I tell him. "I need to find something out."

"Okay."

I walk up to him and kiss him. He kisses me back. He kisses me just the same. Nothing has changed, but I don't feel anything. I don't feel any energy between us. No excitement. No cells reacting. No heat. It is like kissing the backside of your hand.

"Come upstairs with me?" I ask. He smiles. He nods. One look and I can tell he's already hard.

I take him into my bedroom. He undresses quickly. I undress too. We get into my bed and we kiss. I am aware I am kissing him. I am doing the motions. I can do this. This is easy. My body begins to respond. It is not connected to my spirit. This is just a physical thing. This is just my body reacting to stimuli.

I stroke him and tell him to fuck me.

He does.

I abandon my mind and focus on what my body feels and needs. It doesn't take long for me to orgasm. And then I tell him to get out of me. He pulls out. He lies next to me, breathing hard. "I don't want you to finish," I say.

"Okay. I understand."

"I just have a question for you."

"I thought you didn't want to talk."

"I changed my mind."

"Well, I didn't prepare anything to say to your questions."

"You have to prepare? Is that how you manage things? All these women? You prepare answers, come up with a story that sounds plausible?"

"It's not like that. I..."

"What do you want from me? That's my question."

"What do I want from you?"

"Yes. You knew what I wanted going into this. I wanted a monogamous relationship. I was honest and upfront about that. You treated me like your girlfriend. You said we were exclusive. Then when we met up last month, you told me you weren't seeing anyone important. And all this time...all these women...so what did you want? Was it just sex?"

"I guess. Yes. But not all. I...I told you how Marilyn is my best friend. She just gets me and we have so much fun together and..."

"I'm not asking about Marilyn. I'm asking about me. What do you want from me?"

"When I was married, when my wife and I had sex, she'd tell me to just get it over with. To just finish. She was so cold to me and..."

"Again. Not about me."

His penis is soft now. It lies against his leg like a deflated peach balloon. I sit up, not caring about how I look. My soft, full breasts, the rolls of my stomach. We are completely naked and I can see all of my flaws, but I can also see his. I can see exactly who he is.

"I'm not attracted to Marilyn, but I sleep with her. And I need...I love sex, you know? But I don't want it to be just fucking. I don't want someone cold like my wife was. I want the emotion too."

His skin is smooth. Pale. I can see little veins threading just under the surface. He has hardly any muscles. No definition to his shape. He is not particularly handsome. All the glimmer and beauty I once saw in him is gone. He's just a man. And I don't want him in my bed anymore.

I don't want him in my life. I understand him now. He loves Marilyn, but he doesn't want her physically, so he uses other women to meet his sexual needs. I'm just a tool for him to feel sated. I get it. "So, you made me believe we had a relationship so that when we had sex, I'd have emotion for you. You could be adored." This is a man who needs to be the hero. He needs to be worshipped. I think of the many women he's seeing now: of Jen and their upcoming romantic weekend. Of the woman he hasn't slept with...yet. How many women is he talking to currently? He has them at all different stages in a relationship. Some long term, some newly dating, some he's just beginning to know. He figures out what to say, what to do. He is always in that exciting stage of dating and loving someone, when things are new and wonderful. And when they get hard, or he loses his attraction, he breaks up with them, and chooses another.

"I'm not manipulating you. I really want..."

He begins to get excited and I see a flash in his eyes, a change. The way my stepmother would change when she was about to lash out or coerce. He has sized me up and he is about to say what he thinks I want to hear. "I just want to find my person," he says, and smiles.

He has read my blogs. We've had conversations. He is not using *his* words. He is using mine. This pale, naked, limp man in my bed is still trying to manipulate me. He is a narcissist. Maybe psychopathic. He's clearly a sex addict. I think of his poor wife. He must've had affairs, of course he did. How much she had to endure his endless need to be worshipped, adored, to fuck and fuck and fuck and fuck and fuck.

"You're looking for your person?" I say and look him in the eyes.

"Yes!" He smiles.

"I'd like you to pay me for my ticket to the show." I don't ask him for the money for the flight and the hotel. I'm too embarrassed to tell him I upgraded us to First Class. The money I spent on that is lost.

"Oh, no. I don't think so."

"You don't think so?"

"We can still go. I'll be whoever you need to be. Can't you just think about it? I've never been to New York and you know it so well. We can still have a great time. I'm hoping it can still be a passionate twenty-four hours, you know. I was so looking forward to that." He smiles again. Reaches out to trace the skin on my arm. It takes everything in me not to recoil. "Or if you just need to go as friends, we can do that too, but it would be so much more fun if we were more than friends. If we had that passion."

"So you don't want to give me my money back for the ticket? If I don't go, will you still go?"

"Of course, you'll go. We've got the flight and everything. Can you just think about it?" His smile is terrifying.

He's not going to give me the $500 back for the ticket. I either go with him and see the show, or I lose all that money. "You'll act any way I ask you to?"

He nods. Smiling. "Of course. But I'm hoping...It can be like today. Like what we had here. Only I'd have a chance to finish." He laughs. Isn't he charming, with his charming laugh?

I get up. Get dressed.

"Thank you," I say. "Thank you for answering my questions with such honesty. I have to go to work now. Can you let yourself out?"

"Is that...That's it?"

"Yeah. That's it. I'm going to work and then get ready for the party. Let's connect over the weekend so we can figure out where and when to meet for our big trip on Tuesday."

"Ah! Okay. So. We're still going?"

"Of course we're going." I say, and I let my eyes flash too. "I'm so excited."

I don't think he sees the flash. He doesn't know what it means.

He doesn’t really know who he's dealing with.

# 62.The Party

I disconnect from my thoughts and focus on the party. I lose myself in cutting thin slices of brie, placing them tenderly on the puff pastry, spooning on chutney and sprinkling with pecans. I slice meat and cheese for the charcuterie board. I thread tiny plastic swords with cherry tomatoes, basil, and tiny mozzarella balls. I put on my makeup, tell the kids when I'll be home, take my dogs for a walk, and then head over to Erin's.

We get dressed up. We agree not to think about anything but tonight. She won't think of her heartache and I won't think of mine. We smile. We take pictures. Our friends come over. Some of them are nominated for awards, and we watch the live broadcast wishing we were in New York.

I'll be in New York in just a few days, and I'm terrified, but I don't think about it.

We laugh.

I get drunk.

I text the singer I flirted with on Christmas Eve and send him a picture of me in the bathroom and a beam of light shining on my ample cleavage. I am having so much fun. Life is fun and light, and Ryan is not by my side, but it doesn't matter. Nothing matters. I don't matter. Everything is beautiful and made of crystal and my life is exactly the way it should be. I am having exactly the night I should have.

And don't I have the life I should have?

Isn't there something so completely broken and terrible in me that I deserve this life? This fragile life? Don't I deserve a mother who needs me to parent her, an ex who was so depressed he wanted to die. Don't I deserve neglect and lies and hurt and abandonment? Isn't life a whirlwind? A merry-go-round? A work of art?

I eat too much. I laugh too loud. But the pictures we post online are great. The pictures are the only thing that matters.

I have to wait a long time before I'm sober enough to drive home. Erin fills me with food and coffee. She asks if I'm sure I'm all right and I tell her of course I'm sure. Of course I am.

When I get home, I can't sleep, so I stay up late and sit at my computer and I begin to write a blog. In the blog I tell the whole story of what has happened to me.

I tell it because I am tired of being quiet. Because being quiet allows people to keep doing bad things to others. Being quiet makes you complicit. Being quiet means you keep their secrets, and they keep on going. And it isn't fair. Maybe this is the life I deserve. The life I've somehow earned. Fine. I'll take it. But it stops with me.

I send the blog to Erin before posting it, just to be sure. And then I cancel Ryan's ticket to New York. I'll eat the $500 for the show. I am not going with him. If he goes, he'll have to go on his own. He'll have to pay for his flight and his hotel room, and he'll have to find another woman to buy her own ticket. I feel sorry for her and I wish I could warn her, but there isn't time. There isn't energy. All I want to do is sleep.

I text him one more time and say, "I've canceled your flight. I never want to hear from you again."

He immediately responds and says, "What?!?!!!"

Then I block him. From my phone, my computer, my social media, and please, oh please, I block him from my life.

I fall asleep on the couch and sleep for a couple of hours, and am up and moving before the kids.

I don't dream.

# 61. The Numbing

I call Erin in the morning. I'm...concerned.

I can't sleep. I have no appetite. But what scares me, what truly scares me, is I don't feel anything. Well, I feel afraid, but that's it. I can recognize it as fear, but it isn't a true feeling. My heart isn't racing. It's steady. But something is off. Shouldn't I feel something? Shouldn't I cry, scream? Shouldn't I be filled with rage? Shouldn't I be screaming? This man lied to me, outright and boldly. He manipulated me, used me. He hurt me. He *hurt* me. And yet...

He wasn't my husband. He was just someone I thought I loved. He never promised me anything, really. He said we were exclusive, but so what? What should I expect in my late forties? Maybe it's not a big deal. But for the love I felt, shouldn't the absence of that love make me feel something?

But I don't feel. I don't.

I look around calmly and I see the world around me. Here is the stove and my kitchen. Here is the sunlight pouring in through the windows. Here are my hungry dogs. My kids are upstairs and they will be hungry soon too. I should cook something for them. There are lots of things I should do. I should smile and cook pasta Bolognese and ask them about their days. I should laugh at certain moments. I should feel frustrated when we talk about homework and I know I can't help them. I should clean the kitchen when they go upstairs. I should eat some ice cream.

I should maybe feel stressed about all the work I have to do.

I should hurt that this trip I'm supposed to take isn't going to happen. Because it's not going to happen. Clearly. This trip was something I wished for. He was someone I wished for. Maybe these terrible things happened because I wished it so.

I should be grieving over knowing the relationship I thought I had was a carefully constructed lie. Everything I felt wasn't based on reality. What I felt was real, but what he did was lie to me. Consciously. That should hurt, shouldn't it?

Shouldn't I be bereft? Shouldn't I be on my knees? Shouldn't the pain make me crawl into bed and cry?

But I feel fine. I feel okay. I think.

I don't feel angry or sad. I don't feel hurt or happy. I don't feel pain or joy. I could walk over coals or sharp knives and it wouldn't hurt. You could call me any name right now, say any ugly truth to me and I would agree with you and nod. You could lift me off the planet, take me away from everything and everyone I love and that would be fine, really. It would be okay.

This is me breathing in my body. Getting a cup of water. Tasting the cold liquid and making my throat swallow. This is me brushing and flossing my teeth. Hugging my kids. Putting dishes in the dishwasher. This is me talking and breathing and feeling just fine.

"Erin," I say. "I'm fine. I'm totally fine."

"Are you?" she asks. "Because you still don't sound right."

I nod though she can't see me, and then I realize what the fear is. My voice is steady when I say, "The last time I felt this kind of fine was when my stepmother broke a chair and tried to kill me. I know I'm in my body right now, Erin, but I'm not really here. I think that maybe I'm not fine at all."

I know what this is.

It's like my therapist told me so many months ago, to be wary of the man I was attracted to.

I know what this is because I've seen this before. I have held this globe by my fingertips and spun it around, viewing it from all angles.

This is a trauma response.

I've been here before.

I've felt this before.

It's like I told the therapist.

I feel like I am home.

# 62. The Blog

Erin reads the blog and tells me I can't post it. "I love you; you know that. And I know you process things through writing but, honey, you can't post this. You can't."

"Why?" I ask. I really want to know.

"It's so...raw. It's not even that. It's really damning, and I guess it should be. I don't know why exactly. But maybe it's what it could do to you. It feels like revenge. And you aren't a vengeful person. You've got to think about what you share online and getting cast and your career and I'm so sorry. I want to tell you to post this, but I'm scared for you."

I know she's right, but it makes me angry. I am angry because he wins. He wins. How many women has he hurt, and how many times have they been quiet? It isn't fair.

"Is there a way you could...I don't know...change it somehow so you're not the victim, so you're helping instead of hurting?"

"But I am a victim."

"I know you are. I know. But, just, maybe think on it a little bit? Reread it when you're thinking a little more clearly? Whatever you do, I'll support you, but I'm scared for you."

Erin usually doesn't give a fuck, and her tentative approach here scares me and warns me to listen. So I do. I don't post the blog.

Instead, I rewrite it. I don't attack. I simply tell the story. Plainly. And then I submit it to every online source I can. If an editor thinks it has merit, if a publication thinks it's something that women will connect with, if it could somehow help someone, then I'll publish it that way. If no one wants it, then I'll tuck it away.

I hear back from the HuffPost in two hours, asking for a few changes. They'll publish it. Next Tuesday. A week after Ryan flies to New York with someone else.

Of course, it will publish on a Tuesday, but this time I'm okay with it. The truth could reach a much larger audience than I could through my tiny blog, and it's that thought that finally, at long last, allows me to crawl into bed and sleep.

# 63. The Ticket

On Tuesday, at 10:32 p.m. Ryan pays me for the ticket to the show. I know why he waits until 10:32. It's when the show gets out. He pays me then so I will know he went to New York anyway. He took someone with him and he had the romantic twenty-four hours he intended on having. He lifted me right out of that fantasy and put someone else in my place. The particulars of the person didn't matter. He just needed a woman in the space.

That poor woman, I think.

Then I start counting down until the article comes out.

One more week.

Just seven days.

The thought is a tiny ember in my heart that glows. I don't know what fuels it. Anger, maybe, hurt, sadness. I don't question it. I just let that tiny ember heat my heart. I need a little fire in me to get through the next few days.

## 64. The Doctor's Office 2

I spend the morning in the doctor's office, naked from the waist down, waiting for the doctor to come in and perform a series of STI tests on me.

It is humiliating.

I'm told to take off my pants and underwear, wrap myself with a thin sheet, and sit on the exam table.

The humiliation rolls slowly over me, starting with my toes and working its way up my entire body. It's more than the thin gown they give me to cover myself with, or that I'm sitting on a plastic covering on the exam table. It's more than sweating and looking at the instruments that are laid out and ready to go inside of me. It's more than my feet being cold and the time moving so slowly. It's sitting in this cold, sterile room, and realizing I made choices that landed me here. It's a feeling that I did this to myself.

I willfully ignored all the red flags. I justified all the warning signs. I believed in him because I was so sure we had potential. That we had a future. It's humiliating that I believed that. How stupid of me. How utterly reckless and foolish. I should know better. Shame on me for allowing myself to feel for him.

This experience is my fault.

I trusted Ryan. I loved him. *I* did this to *myself.*

But, of course, logically I know, I didn't. I loved him. I believed in him. That shouldn't be a bad thing. That should be a beautiful thing. To be open and vulnerable, even after so many heartbreaks, should be a thing of triumph.

***

I have been sitting here naked and vulnerable for a lifetime.

I wonder if the doctor has forgotten about me, and that is when it happens.

The ice around me starts to melt, and I feel yanked firmly into my body, from the space where I have been floating outside it.

I am in my body, cold, in this doctor's office, waiting to know if I am okay.

It is a quiet cry, but it is shattering.

It is a cry from deep in my gut, deep in my bones. It is a cry of not having control, of being hurt, of being violated. I cry not because this man hurt me emotionally, but because of his lies and his choices, because I believed him, I might have contracted something that will affect my entire life, and perhaps prevent me from ever finding a partner. He has had unprotected sex with many, many women and because I slept with him, because I trusted him, I could be sick.

I cry because I am a victim of something that isn't even considered a crime.

He took away the control I had over my body. He stole that from me.

I can't breathe from the crying. I can't breathe, but I can feel.

When the doctor enters the room, she says, "Well, honey, did you find out he cheated on you?" I nodded because I can't speak. "I see it all the time," she says. She gently leads me through the exam while I try to hold my emotions in long enough to get through it.

After the exam, she asks if I need anything else. "I'm not sleeping. Can we double my Trazadone for a while? And can you give me a prescription for a Xanax or something?"

"We can do those things," she says. "Are you going to see someone? Do you have support?"

"I have friends. I'm seeing my therapist in a few days. And, funny thing, I wrote an article that's going to be published by the HuffPost next week."

Her smile is wide. "You did? Good for you! More people need to talk about this. I see this all the time. Women who come in needing to be tested because their partners are cheating on them." Hearing this hurts my heart. I'm not the only one. Of course I'm not the only one. What is happening to me is commonplace. It makes me sick.

"If you had to give just one piece of advice to women, what would it be?" I ask.

"Easy. I'd tell everyone to get tested yearly for STIs. Make it part of your routine. People do bad things, even people we love." She pats my knee and the little bit of kindness makes the tears start again. "Take all the time you need in here. I'm glad you have friends and a therapist. Keep talking about this. And I'll put in those prescription requests."

***

I will have two days of agonizing waiting. Of checking my online account to see which tests have come in, and which haven't. Am I okay? I feel okay. He was so particular about me being tested before we had sex and became 'exclusive' that my one hope left is he was that particular with everyone. *Please, please let him have been paranoid enough.*

The tests start to come in. I'm negative, negative, negative until one test comes back with an exclamation point. My heart stops as I read the result.

I'm positive for Hepatitis B.

This man, this absolute predator, has ruined my life.

# 65. Texts

ERIN: Wait. What? WHAT? This isn't text material. This is phone call material.
ME: I can't talk.
ME: ...
ME: ...
ME: I mean I physically can't talk.
ERIN: I'm here. Whatever you need. I'm here.

***

ME: Tested positive for Hepatitis B. Dr. says it's a recent infection so you likely passed it on to me on one of the two times we were together last month. I was tested back in April for everything before we became intimate the first time and you have been my only sexual partner. You have ruined my life.
RYAN:Oh my. I'll go get tested immediately.

***

ME: Have you been having sex with men too? I have not received my HIV test result yet and I am truly terrified. What is my risk? I'm scared.
RYAN: Oh my goodness no
ME: You have lied to me about everything. How can I trust you?
RYAN:...
RYAN:...
RYAN:...

***

ERIN: I looked it up. Hep B. What it means. What it could mean. Fuck.
Fuck! Are they sure?
ME: Weirdly the doctor says there are some questions.
ERIN: What questions?
ME: I don't understand it all but it's flagging as the virus is present, but the 2nd test says it's not confirmed.
ERIN: What does that mean? Is there a chance it's wrong?
ME: I don't know.

***

ME: I'm sorry to send another email but I'm very concerned about the test results. It's been three days. I thought results would be ready in 48 hours. I also haven't heard yet from the HIV test. Am I positive? Is your office waiting to call me? If someone could call me to talk about this, I'd appreciate it. I'm going out of my mind with worry.

DR: Other tests negative. Waiting for confirmation on HEP B.

ME: Does that mean the HIV test is back and I'm negative?

DR: ...

DR: ...

DR: ...

***

ME: I hate you. I hate everything about you. Every moment we knew each other, you lied to me. The first time we met. When you said you hadn't connected with anyone the way you connected with me? A lie. You saw your girlfriend that same night. When you read my blog about "The Tuesday Girl" and I told you how I felt like a Tuesday Girl to you and you said it made you cry, reading that. You told me how much you cared about me. That I wasn't just some fling on the side. You could have told me right then. I WAS a fling on the side. You lied. You could've let me know. But you lied! You never cared about me. You took away my hope and my belief in love. You hurt me. You made me sick. You went from my bed to someone else's and then someone else's and then someone else's and you...You lied. Every moment. You hurt me. YOU HURT ME! YOU MADE ME SICK! And you're still doing it. To other women. Do you understand? Do you have any sense of how truly vile you are? DO YOU? What is wrong with you?

How fucking broken are you? Your boys. What are you teaching them? How could you do this?

ME: (delete delete delete. You can't send that text. He won't actually care.

And it won't change anything. It will only make you look ugly and unhinged even though you have every right to be ugly and unhinged.)

***

ERIN: Anything yet?
ME: Nothing.
ERIN: Fuck. How long has it been?
ME: Four days.
ERIN: How long til you know?
ME: They said this test could take 3 weeks.
ERIN: FUCK!!!
ME: Oh wait! I just got a text. A new result is in.
ERIN: GO READ IT

***

DR: HIV neg. All other tests STI negative. No HEP B virus confirmed in your body. It seems like you might be a "reactor." Sorry for the scare. No need to follow up unless your liver goes crazy or something.

***

ME: Call me.
ERIN: Okay.

***

ME: I got some news today. I had two positive results to hepatitis B but the deeper tests show no actual infection. My doctor believes that I am a reactor to the test and not actually infected. I don't know if this scare will affect you at all, but the last thing I want to say to you is that this should show you how easy it is to get an STI and pass it on to others. By lying to me about being exclusive, you took away my choice and control with my body and the number of partners I'm exposed to. You're a hypocrite. You say you are an advocate for women's health, and taking the choice away from me is wrong. Please, if you have any sense of decency, please tell your partners that you are sexually active with multiple people. Let them make the choice whether they are okay with that. You took that from me. I will never forgive you for that. I never want to hear from you or see you again.

RYAN:...
ME: <BLOCKED>

***

Call:

Erin calls me and I answer. I don't say anything, I just answer.

"Hi," she says.

I choke a little on the words. I still can't speak. It hurts. It's hard.

She says, "It's okay. I'm here. You're okay, yeah? You're okay!"

"I'm okay," I finally manage. "But, Erin, I'm not really okay."

"I know. Of course you're not. But you will be. You will be."

She stays on the phone with me until my breathing evens and my throat unlocks.

"I love you," she says.

When I can speak again, I say words that are healing. "I love you too."

# 66. The Truth Is

I'm sitting at Erin's kitchen island. We've just run out to pick up lunch, poke bowls loaded with shrimp and rice and marinated mushrooms. It is soothing food. Nourishing.

"Okay, so what's the news? I'm not sure I can handle much more. Please tell me you're okay. Nothing else earth-shattering, right?"

"Nope. Things are okay. But I've made some decisions."

"Okay. Hit me. I'm ready."

"I decided I can sit in misery and blame myself for being stupid and vulnerable and loving, or I can do something different. There's something about these last two years on my own that has changed something in me. Have you noticed it? It feels like an actual shift in my DNA. I am not the person I was before."

"You're not. But I think this new person was always there, just beneath the surface."

I nod. Take a bite. It's so good. "Right. If what happened to me with Ryan had happened even a few years ago, I'd have pontificated on what was so wrong and broken in me. Why did I deserve this? Why me? But I don't feel that way now."

"What do you feel? You are feeling again?"

I nod. Smile a little. "I am starting to feel and it surprises me. I feel angry. I feel empowered."

"Yes," she says. "This is good, yeah?"

I nod. It is good. I keep going: "So you know I wrote that blog about my experience with him because I feel like what I went through is a secret. It's not my secret. It's Ryan's secret. And I hate fucking secrets."

"Yeah. Clearly. Your family was all about the secrets."

"Yes! And he can keep treating women this way because the women he dates are kind and considerate. They don't want to expose him because it's embarrassing. They don't tag him on social media because they're considerate. They don't call him out because they're kind. And this is how he controls women and gets away with being cruel. Keeping this secret only protects him and festers inside of me. And it isn't right. I am not the broken one here. He is."

Erin is nodding and smiling.

"While I have regrets about my marriages ending (or failing) I don't feel they ended because I'm broken. They ended because I'm strong."

"Yeah, of course."

"And I didn't deserve this experience. I thought I did, but that's not true. That's what people who abuse you want you to think. That you deserve it. It's another way they can control you. The real truth is...There isn't anything in me that invited this to happen. This is his secret. Not mine. And I do not need to keep it."

Erin is teary eyed. "Okay. So who are you going to tell?"

I take a breath. "I thought about the blog, and you're right. I can't publish it. But I thought if I submitted it to some established places, if they thought there was something valuable there, if they published it, then it wouldn't be about me attacking Ryan. It would be something that could help other women. So I rewrote the blog and submitted it to the HuffPost. Within two hours, I heard back from them. They're asking for a few revisions and then they're publishing it. Tomorrow."

There is a pause in the kitchen. No sound at all. Then Erin explodes. She jumps off her stool and dances around. "Holy fucking shit! The balls on you! Or I should say, the size of your ovaries!! The HuffPost? Who does that? Who writes an article and says fuck this shit, here you go HuffPost and Huff Post says, hell yes, we're going to print that shit. I mean, holy hell!"

I nod.

I'm smiling too. "You were right. If I posted it to my blog it would be vindictive, and that's not who I want to be, but if someone picked it up, then there'd be some validation this is a story that needs to be told. I mean, I'm not the girlfriend, but I feel like this perspective is important too. So many times, people blame the other woman for 'stealing' a man, but what if she doesn't even know? It's not the woman's fault. It's not my fault. It's his. And I want people to know that predators like this exist."

"Fucking A." She sits back down. "Are you going to use his name?"

I shake my head. "That's the only thing. They've asked me to change his name and some identifying details. But everything I'm telling is true. And even if he never reads it, I just feel like it's important that I put it out there."

"Damn," she says. Then "damn" again.

We eat our poke bowls. We have coffee. We sit on her back porch and watch the birds in the woods, two squirrels chasing each other.

A half hour later, Erin says, "Fucking A. Fucking A."

# 67. The Article

The following Tuesday, I'm nervous. I've had things published before, so it's not that. This is a different nervous. They let me know when it posts, and I share it on my social media feeds. It makes me nauseous, posting about this, but I do it anyway. And I tell my friends to share it.

They do.

The piece gets two hundred thousand views in the first twelve hours. I get messages sent to me on Facebook, Instagram, through my website. They say *Me too, this is happening to me, Thank you for writing this. I thought I was the only one to be duped.* Women ask me for his picture and his real name. They send pictures of their own. *Is this him? Is this Ryan?*

Everyone tells me not to read the comments, but of course I do. It's what I expect, but it saddens me all the same. How could I be so stupid, obviously this guy was a con artist. But there are meaner comments, things like you should've just been happy with what you had. *Two marriages? Two divorces? Hello, red flags. A woman your age isn't going to find anyone to share her life with.* They comment on my appearance, my weight, but most of all my age. *She should know better. She's in her forties and still falling for shit like this? This woman is pathetic.*

There seems to be a hatred of women in general, but especially for women who have the audacity of wanting more, of wanting love in their later life, of wanting healthy relationships, of not staying with the man who deigned to marry her.

But there are responses posted on the comments, readers who say Blaming the victim, typical, and She's beautiful, and This could happen to anyone.

I reach out to Marilyn and let her know I published an article. I say that I kept it from my point of view and I hope she understands. She writes back that she read it and she hopes I find someone who will love me. I tell her she deserves the same.

Then it's over.

It's done.

My life was hijacked for a while, but it's okay now. I can get back to it.

I sign into a dating app. It feels reckless, yes, but I do it because he doesn't get to hurt me so much I stop trying or believing in companionship. He doesn't get any more space or time from my life.

I move on.

I move the fuck on.

# 68. Stop It

I'm pacing in my kitchen, earbuds in, talking on the phone, making loops around the island. During the pandemic, there were people who ran marathons in their house and I'm starting to wonder if I'll get a medal. It's cold outside, bitter, with the kind of wind that hits you in the face and steals your breath, so I'm not doing my walk today, and I really need to do my walk. I feel unmoored. Again. My mind and heart swirling.

I know I'm still not okay with everything I've been through, but I don't know how to change that. I'm too embarrassed to go back to my therapist, because she warned me Ryan was a walking red flag, and I'm too ashamed to go to my life coach because I believed in the glass of marbles and I could have anything I asked for. I asked. And this is what has happened to me.

I've been chatting with men. I've met a couple, but it's not working. It's just not. And I know the real reason why is that I'm not working. There's something broken in me. I just don't know what it is or how to fix it.

Erin listens patiently while I rant.

"I mean, what am I doing wrong?" I ask her. I'm speaking fast. My heart is revving. Everything is sped up, when only a week ago, everything was in slow motion. I keep trying to explain. "I'm so confused. I had yet another guy tell me I'm A Lot. He looked me up online, researched me, which is fine, I researched him too. He read the article and thought I was really brave and whatever. That's not what he had a problem with. He looked up the stuff I've done in my career and the things I've accomplished, which in the grand scheme of things really doesn't mean shit. I'm a nobody. No one cares how many books I've recorded or written, but for some reason, it's intimidating to men. And we had a great conversation and he said I'm a lot and then nothing. No text, no email, just silence.

"And the same thing happened with the German guy I had coffee with. We laughed and had a great conversation. He was really cute. Like he didn't hijack my system, which I know is a red flag, but he was cute enough that I thought, this one I could get excited about. This one I could talk to for a while, hang out with. This one, I'm curious about what he looks like naked. Maybe. Eventually. And then after our coffee, we walked through the snow and slush and ice to the building his mom just sold. It's now a cheese shop. We peered in through the windows, looking at the signs of fromage on the walls, and it started to snow and it was a nice moment, you know? It was nice? He gave me a hug, we went our separate ways. He texted me on the app to say he enjoyed meeting me, I responded and gave him my number. And you know what? He unmatched from me. He fucking ghosted me! No reason given. Nothing. Just gone.

"And then today, I'm chatting with this guy who is adorable and we're making plans to meet and he says, I need to tell you something. He says I have a girlfriend and we've been in a relationship for five years. It's an open relationship. She sees other people, and so do I. We're really open about it with each other. So what I'm looking for is someone to be passionate with in between the times I see her.

"My heart stopped. It fucking stopped in my chest.

"Here is yet another man saying, you are attractive and I'm interested in you, but you're not attractive enough. You're not good enough. You're only kinda good. You're good enough to fuck, but not be in a relationship with."

I pause to pour some water. "I'm not peeing," I say. "Just getting water."

"Okay. It's fine if you're peeing though," Erin says, "Anything else?"

"Yes! And the last guy I was talking to looked at my stuff, isn't intimidated by what I do, says I seem fun and then says it's too bad I'm not looking for casual. A-FUCKING-GAIN. Too bad I don't want to just fuck him and am looking for an actual relationship. Another guy I'm not good enough for. I don't deserve a relationship. I'm not good enough for that. What the fuck am I doing wrong? I don't understand! I AM FULLY BEING ME. I AM OPEN HEARTED AND VULNERABLE AND HONEST AND TRUE AND THERE IS SOMETHING BROKEN IN ME AND I WANT TO FIX IT, I DO, I'M TRYING BUT I DON'T KNOW WHAT THAT THING IS!" I'm panting now. Surely, I've hit the halfway point in the marathon. "And let's just say, hypothetically, that I meet someone and I like them and they like me back. How am I ever going to trust anyone ever again after what Ryan did to me? How? HOW?

It hurts. It really does. I want to get better, but I don't even know how I'm sick.

"Erin, please," I say. "Help me. And don't tell me that when I stop looking for love, I'll find it. I know you won't say that, but so many people tell me that I want to punch them. You know what happens when I stop looking? Nothing! Because I work from home. Because of this fucking Covid. I'm home alone all the time. If I'm not looking for a relationship, no one is going to find me. And I'm going mad with loneliness. I just want someone to sit on the couch with me and hold my hand. We don't even have to talk. We don't have to have anything in common. Just fucking hold my hand. Just touch me so I know I exist. That I'm important too. But that can't even happen because I'm broken. No one wants to spend time with me. There's something un-loveable in me, and I don't know how to fix it."

The house ticks.

I wait for her to say something. She doesn't.

"Erin?"

I can hear her breathing. And I know it's coming. Something seismic. Something earth-shattering. Something that is true and I am not prepared. I'm not. But I need to know.

She takes a deep breath. "Did it ever occur to you that maybe you should just fucking stop? I mean, Christ, STOP. It's so exhausting. You must be worn out. Listen to me! There is nothing wrong with you. You don't have to fix fucking ANYTHING! It's not you. It's these guys and wherever they're at. They're not for you. It doesn't mean you're broken; it just means they're not enough for you. Just stop. I watch you spinning your wheels, going to therapy, blogging about all this, sitting in this soup of misery, contemplating what you can change and you don't need to fucking change anything! Goddammit! JUST STOP! If I was a man and I read your blog, I'd think, so, she's hot and fun but she's got some major stuff happening. She doesn't have room in her life for me, so maybe later."

I don't know how to process what she's said. I'm trying but my brain isn't quick enough. "You're telling me to stop writing my blog?"

"No, I'm just telling you to stop. In general. Stop. Stop changing. Stop growing. Stop fixing. I look at you sometimes and I think, God she's so awesome. Why does she hate herself so much? Why is she doing this? And you asked me what is wrong with you. You want the truth. I'm telling you. What is wrong with you is fucking nothing. Stop trying. Just take a break. If one guy doesn't want you, that's his fucking loss. Move on. I know a relationship is important to you. Fuck, we all need connection, and maybe you need it a little more right now. I know you don't have family and you spend your time alone when your kids aren't with you, and there isn't someone to check in with you as a woman instead of as a mom. But you are awesome. You have so much to offer. So just stop with this bullshit already. Just fucking stop. It's exhausting. You don't need to fix anything. You need to just stop."

I truly don't understand.

"But what will I do?" My voice is childlike. "What do I do if I'm not trying to fix myself?"

"I don't know. Maybe...maybe you just live. Maybe you just live your big, fucking beautiful life."

# 69. Living

At first, I'm really fucking angry at Erin and what she said to me. But then...

Then...

It's like stepping into a cold lake. At first the water shocks you, chills you so much it almost hurts, but then your body gets used to it, so you move in another foot or so. And the same thing happens when you reach your knees, your waist, your breasts: there's a shock, the hurt, the chill, and then your body adjusts.

This is what happens to me.

I sit in the chaos of my emotions and I try to take what Erin said to me into my body. Of all the people on the planet, I trust her the most. She wouldn't say something to hurt me. She's saying what she believes, that I need to stop, and she said it the only way she could to ensure I'd listen. There was so much noise around me, it was the only way to hear her.

I hear her.

What if I stopped?

What if I stopped trying to fix myself? Stopped trying to be perfect. What if I didn't need everyone's approval or admiration or love? What if I could calmly move through my life, breathing in the good things that happen to me, and breathing past the hurtful ones.

What if I stopped trying?

What if I just...*was*?

I close my dating apps, and I book a trip to see Lynn, my roommate from college. She's been asking me to go to Colorado, and I have one more tiny window of time left where the kids' dad can take them, before he leaves on a seven month hike on the Pacific Trail. I can take one more small respite and figure out some shit. Figure out my shit.

***

I have two days in Denver by myself before Lynn picks me up. I use those two days to just be. I sleep. I sleep hard. I go to restaurants by myself. I get an appetizer, a drink. I savor the food, the wine.

I stumble on a bar with a live jazz trio. It's their first time playing since Covid and there's an air of celebration to it. I sit at the bar and listen to the music. Feel it. Soak it in. I love live jazz so much, and this is a special gift. While sitting at the bar, I type a tiny poem into my phone, and it seems to summarize everything I've been feeling.

How heartsad I must've been
To accept the crumbs you gave me
And then thank you for the cake.

I have been heartsad for a long time. For my whole life. And I have accepted the smallest morsels of kindness and affection and called that love. But it hasn't been love, and it hasn't been enough to sustain me.

The person who needs to sustain me...is me.

It's in the boundaries I set with dating and how I allow myself to be treated. It's in the friendships I develop and savor. It's in building a solid relationship with my kids that is based on safety and comfort and love. It's the food and drink I put in the body, how I move through the world, the things I give my time and energy to.

On my last night on my own, I go to a fancy restaurant. It's a Saturday and they have a four-course tasting menu. I order that. When they ask who is joining me, I say no one, and I smile. They seat me at a table where I can see the entire restaurant. I order a glass of wine and move my way through the tasting menu. It's fantastic and beautiful. I order a wedge salad, fresh bread, a lobster bisque. I have whitefish balanced on a bed of potatoes in a bright yellow curry sauce, and I end the meal with toffee pudding so rich and decadent it feels like Christmas morning. It feels like I'm on a date with myself, and I'm not sure I've ever felt that.

The next morning, Lynn picks me up. We talk for hours, walk in gardens, and around her house. We go to museums and art stores. She's scheduled in an afternoon nap for me, and each day I nap. We go to a spa. We drink artisanal cocktails and order dessert wherever we go. It's all indulgent and wonderful and so soul soothing.

There's one man I'm still chatting with, but in a relaxed way. He shows me pictures of the foraging he does. The mushrooms he's found, the meals he's cooked over the campfire. He shares pictures of Michigan woods, and I begin to long for home.

When I leave Denver, I leave changed.

I've decided that Erin is right. There is nothing wrong with me. I don't have to prove anything. There are people in my life who love me exactly as I am, the way that I love them.

I can fill my life with good things. With music, and food, with hikes, with adventure, with laughter, with companionship. I don't have to fight for these things, or ask for them. These are things that have always been available to me, and I just never knew it.

My aunt has told me over the years, "You can't know at twenty what you know at forty."

I know so much more now.

I have been so unkind to myself over the years. I have been unkind to others.

I decide the only thing I really need to change is my perspective.

And so I do.

# 70. BOUNDARIES

Something curious happens to me in the coming months. I begin to set boundaries. I'd been toying with them over the years, but the struggle to actually do it lessens. It starts with a conversation with my kiddo, Locust.

"Mom," they say one morning over vegetarian sausage patties and croissants. "I don't want to go between houses anymore."

I sip my coffee. "Okay," I say, "tell me more. What does that mean?"

"It means that I just want one house. I want to stay here."

"You'll be here for seven months soon when your dad goes on his trip." He leaves in June and won't be back until December.

"I know," they say. "But I don't want it to be just for his trip. I want it to be forever. And I want it to start now."

I nod. I get it. I do. "Okay. So, we'll tell your dad."

Locust's face turns red. "I don't want to tell him. How do I do that? It's going to make him mad, and I don't want him to be mad at me."

I react emotionally first. Their dad will be mad, but not at Locust. He'll be mad at me. He'll say I manipulated the kids, got them to change their minds. He'll think I'm a bad person. He'll blame me. He'll...

But it doesn't matter what he thinks, does it? This isn't about him. It's not about me either. And whatever I tell Locust now will have reverberations in their life. What kind of life do I want my kiddo to lead?

I think about the mental illness in my family. The heartbreak. The dysfunction. These patterns are easy to continue because they are known. What is harder, is stopping them.

My Locust has the power to create the life they want to lead, simply by staying strong about their own needs. So, instead, I tell them this, "You're not responsible for your dad's feelings. I don't think he's not going to be mad, and even if he is, that's okay. That's his stuff. It's probably more accurate to say he'll be hurt and disappointed, but that's to be expected. I'd be hurt and disappointed. That's just being a human and a parent. But, honey, you can't live your life for other people. Whatever choices you make, whatever actions you do, if they're based on how others react or how they will feel, then what you do will never be enough. You have to live the best life you can for yourself. Right now, you're saying you need stability. That's something you need. That's valid. Your dad will adjust."

It hits me in the gut when I say Locust shouldn't live for other people. In mothering Locust, I'm mothering some part of myself. I have lived my life so long for others that part of me disappeared, and no matter what I did, it was never enough. It caused a lot of pain for me later when I realized what I was doing and tried to change. If from the very start, I'd said no to some things, how would my life be different?

The truth is, when you live for other people and try to make them happy, whatever you

do can never be enough. They will always want more from you. I don't want Locust to live that way.

"Tell me a little bit more about why you want to stay here," I say.

"It's just that I feel like I'm floating, always between the two houses. And I just want something stable, something solid, you know?"

"I do know. I get it. So how about this? How about we schedule an appointment with your therapist, your dad, and me, and we can meet and talk about it. You can tell your dad your decision, have the therapist there to mediate a little, and give him time to process it. I promise you he's going to understand. He's going to come around because he loves you."

I have no doubt of that.

I can see Locust take a deep breath. "Also, everything at their house is temporary. They're getting ready for their big hike on that Pacific Trail or whatever and they've downsized everything. They only thing left is boxes of power bars and some soulless pictures on the wall."

"Soulless?"

"One says I Live for Coffee and the other is Life's a Beach."

I try not to laugh, but it's funny. Locust has a contempt for modern things. She prefers antique pictures, the paintings we have on our walls, the velvet pillows. The types of pictures at her dad's house would drive them crazy. "Okay, so the temporary thing I get, and your dad leaving to go on this big trip, I get, but maybe we don't have to share all the information. Maybe we don't mention the pictures. Maybe we'll just tell him you need something permanent."

Locust smiles then. They put their dish in the sink and give me a quick hug.

It doesn't feel like a huge conversation. It feels everyday. And maybe that's what makes it so big.

Locust doesn't have to live their life for their dad or for me or anyone else.

And I don't have to either. I just need to live for me.

***

My mom calls me while I'm narrating and leaves three messages in the span of five minutes. "I don't understand why you never call me back. I need to talk to you, and you just ignore me."

Then I get a text message from my uncle Pete. "Your mom is trying to contact you, but you haven't responded. Could you give me a call?"

A few minutes after my mom's messages and my uncle's text, I call my uncle. He says my mom has been trying to contact me. "Yes. I saw that. I was in the booth, recording. And she only gave me a few minutes to respond."

"I know," he says. "Yeah. That makes a lot of sense. Listen..." I hear talking in the background. "So, I'm with your mom now and she wants to know if she can have a garage sale at your house. She says she'll take care of everything, but we have to get her things out of storage. We can't afford that expense anymore. So your mom wants to know if we can bring the stuff to you, have a garage sale, and then be done with it."

The whole idea causes my entire body to flare. On the surface, this seems reasonable, but I've been through things like this with my mom before. She's a hoarder. She can't give up her stuff. She wants to bring her stuff to my house, and fill my garage, and keep it here. In many ways, it's a metaphor for our whole relationship. Over the years, my mom has asked me to carry her stuff, to keep it, to shoulder it, and I simply can't do it anymore. If there is a garage sale, I'll have to run it. And I'll have to have my mom here and soothe her and take care of her. This isn't something I want to do.

I tell my uncle no. "I know this is going to sound cruel to you, and I can't help that. But I can't take this on. My mom's stuff is her stuff. Her choices. She's got to take care of it on her own. I can't bring it into my life."

My uncle Pete says okay and he'll let her know. I'm terrified he'll be angry with me and tell me he won't be my uncle anymore. Setting boundaries is scary. It means losing people, and I have so few family members in my life now that losing my uncle feels especially scary. But I can't keep doing this.

That night, he sends me a text. "I was with your mom when I called, but I want you to know that I agree with you. It's just stuff. I'm proud of you. I'm not too good with people but I've always admired you, and I think you're right saying no to your mom. I'll take the stuff to the dump. I'll take care of everything."

I almost can't breathe at the miracle of it. I said no, and my uncle still loves me. More than that, he respects me. I respect myself.

***

I've been texting a few men, thinking about meeting them. I haven't given up on love and to not date anymore feels like letting Ryan win. I will not give him the power to hurt me anymore, and I deserve a partner in my life.

One man likes hiking and the outdoors. He's more active than I am. He runs, kayaks, rock climbs, but he doesn't seem to mind that I'm really just into hiking. He lives a few hours away and says the distance to him is no big deal. We plan for him to come and meet me for lunch. Before we meet, he texts me to say honestly, the distance is an issue for a relationship, but he finds me very physically attractive from my pictures and would I be up for just a physical relationship? An occasional passionate night? It hurts to read this. Another man who just wants me physically, but at the same time, at least this guy was up front about it. I thank him for the honesty and tell him I'm worth more than just an occasional tryst.

Another man is a writer and wants to meet, but he stops texting abruptly. Two weeks later, he reaches out again and apologizes.

Sometimes he just goes off grid. I thank him for reaching back out, but I'm not interested. I need someone in my life who is consistent.

It gets easier and easier to say no to these men. To weed out the ones who don't treat me well. Like Erin has said, in courting, they are on their best behavior and if their best behavior is bad...it ain't ever going to get better.

There is one man I'm really interested in. The one I started chatting with while I was in Denver. He mushroom-hunts, barbecues, is interested in canning and preserving. He's tapped trees for maple syrup, canned fish that he's caught, made jams and pickles. He cuts trees for fun. He has a cabin in the woods and lives on a lake. He has two adult kids. His words are kind and consistent. He makes me laugh with his observations, the way he chats with me. It's playful. Engaging.

We talk mushrooms and cooking. He researches me online and finds the article I wrote for the HuffPost. He tells me he found it and says he hopes I haven't given up on all men. He says what Ryan did was terrible and he's sorry I went through that, but not all men are like that. "Some of us actually want a monogamous relationship. Some of us find that fulfilling."

I want to believe him. I do believe him.

I want to meet this man but when I ask, he hedges. He's not sure if he can. "No problem," I say. "If you're not able to meet, I get it. I'm not interested in a texting-only relationship. I want something real and in person. So, I'm going to back out."

Months ago, I'd have said it was okay, and kept talking to him, waited to see when he could work me into his schedule.

He apologizes. "My dad just had open heart surgery. I should have told you, but we're in this place where we're just getting to know each other. I want to meet you. I do. I phrased everything wrong. Let me see what I can do." He arranges for his sister to stay with his dad for a couple of hours, and we meet on a cold morning for breakfast. He brings me chaga tea that he foraged. He has a long beard and he's impossibly tall.

"You look like a lumberjack," I say.

He smiles.

He has a nice smile.

***

Locust tells her dad that she's going to live with me, and her dad accepts it. It hurts him, I can tell, but Locust's choice is also a result of choices he made in his life. Instead of making his home comfortable, he's stripped it bare. He's leaving for half of a year.

He and his wife have asked me to take care of the kids while they hike, and while I don't agree with their choice to go now, while I think they could wait another two years until the kids are done with school, I tell him of course will take care of my kids. I am already taking care of my kids.

I ask him to help financially a little with groceries for the next few months, since he won't be around at all. I ask him for $200.00 a month. He hedges. He says since our parenting time is equal, I really should only ask for three months of assistance. I ask for three months, and $150.00. He won't even do that. "That's not in our budget," he said, and besides, his wife won't be on board with that.

I accept that. But it niggles at me.

I think of leaving him all those years ago and how I was so afraid of losing the kids, I didn't ask for anything. I had been a stay-at-home mom and he controlled the finances. He said he'd take me to court, and he'd get full custody, so I did everything I could to ensure I'd have access to my kids. I asked for nothing except the car. Over the last decade, I've been so accommodating, so understanding, to the point he's taken advantage of me. And that needs to stop.

Three months into his hike, I ask him again for some financial support. Groceries are expensive. So is gas, electricity, etc. He says no.

I meet with an attorney, and I file a petition for child support. It takes every ounce of strength I have to do it, but I do it. It isn't right that he's checking out early on parenting, and while I can't change his choices, I can advocate for the kids. I can advocate for myself. The attorney crunches numbers. She says she thinks we can ask for $700.00 a month for the next two years, and I can get formal physical full custody.

$700.00 a month for two years. I had been willing to accept $150.00 for three months.

To hear from my attorney that what I was asking for wasn't too much, to hear her say that a parent is accountable for financial support, is so affirming. All I'm asking for is what is fair and just.

My ex calls me from the trail. "How could you do this? I told everyone you were such a wonderful person to take the kids for us."

"Stop there," I say. "I am a wonderful person. My asking for financial support doesn't mean I'm a bad person. It's what is fair."

"But you don't even need it. You probably make more money than I do."

"What I make isn't the issue. I'm parenting full time. Our agreement was for shared custody. I tried a number of times to talk to you about this and you said no. Now we can let the courts decide what is fair. If they think I'm asking for too much, they'll adjust the amount."

"I just don't understand," he says. "You've never done anything like this before."

I agree with him. I haven't. "It's long past time," I say.

# 71. Living a Big, Beautiful Life

When we get a break in the winter weather, and it warms up enough that the ice starts to drip, I call Erin to go for a walk. She says *no fucking way*, so we compromise: she agrees to walk from her warm car in a parking lot to an equally warm restaurant. So, we choose one of our favorite places in downtown Grand Rapids where they have bread service. Erin orders bread pudding for an appetizer, because it's part of her life philosophy: start with the good stuff.

"How's the big, beautiful living going?" she asks me. She kind of knows the answer to this, since we talk every day and I've already filled her in on everything, but I like that she asks. We're sorta fighting over the crème anglaise that the bread pudding is sitting in. Well, not fighting, it's more like our bread pudding-ed forks are skating through it. It's kinda pretty.

"I think it's going well. Today, I made waffles for breakfast."

"That's a good start. Did you slather it in butter and maple syrup?"

I shake my head. "Just butter. I don't like syrup."

"Now see," she says, "it's clear you need some practice on living a big life. Make sure you get real maple syrup, not that corn syrup processed bullshit. That's the first step."

"Okay," I say. "I'll make a note."

We talk about our week, our work, what's on our schedules. She hasn't heard from her ex. She talks about him a lot, the anger still right at the surface. You don't even have to scratch to get to it, it's just right there. I remember when I was in that space. Anger is a good place to start. It can energize you to transform your life, but anger can also stop you from transforming. It can keep you anchored to a shore you don't want to be tied to. She's anchored right now, but I hope soon she'll be able to let go and move on.

"These boundaries you're setting," Erin says. "Holy shit. It's fucking incredible. I mean, look where you were six months ago, and now?"

"I know," I said. "Something happened inside me. I don't know what or how or when exactly. Maybe I grew a pair of balls."

"No," Erin said. "You grew a pair of ovaries. Ovaries the size of fucking fists."

"Yeah," I said. "That's closer to the truth. I have fists in my uterus."

It sounds kinda creepy, but I like this idea. That there's power nestled right inside me.

Maybe it was always there, and I just didn't know.

"It's getting easier," I say. "But it's still hard."

"Yep. Disappointing people is hard. But disappointing yourself? That's tragic."

I nod. I've learned this the hard way.

I ask her something I've been thinking about. "What do you think a trauma-free life is like?" I ask her this honestly. She had a good upbringing and is close with her family. There was pain and all of that, but compared to how I was raised, she had a normal childhood and adolescence. I don't know what a trauma-free life is like, and I'd like to.

"Hmm." She thinks about it. The server takes the bread pudding and replaces it with just plain bread. We both moan. "A trauma-free life? I'm pretty sure it's all popsicles and candy canes and shit."

"Crème brulée and bread pudding."

"It's like high fives and it's always seventy-five degrees and not humid."

"Could we say it's sixty-five degrees and not humid?" I prefer the cold.

She nods. "Yep. I'll wear a sweater. There are birds singing everywhere and we're both fabulously wealthy and well adjusted."

"So, what you're saying is a trauma-free life is pretty boring?"

She nods. "Yes. Exactly. But at least there are waffles."

I laugh at that and then I tell her something else I've been thinking about. "You know that whole 'loving yourself' thing? I've had so many people tell me that you have to love yourself before you can love someone else, and it just makes me angry."

"Okay. I think I get it. Tell me more," she says.

"I do love myself. I've always loved myself. When you tell someone to love themselves it's sort of like you're blaming them. It feels like the shitty things that happen to you or the bad relationships or experiences you've had are because you didn't love yourself enough, and that's not fair. Your ex cheated. He didn't cheat because you didn't love yourself. He cheated because he's a dick. And Ryan didn't lie to me because I don't love myself. He lied to me and manipulated me because he's selfish and cruel. I do love myself. That's not the issue. The issue is I don't know how to be loved by others."

Erin nods, thinking. "It's like that poem you wrote. The one about the crumbs? What is it again?"

I think for a second to remember the wording. "How heartsad I must've been to accept the crumbs you gave me and then thank you for the cake."

"Yep. I tell that to my other friends all the time. When they're talking about the shitty experiences they're having in relationships, I just say *crumbs.* It's not cake, honey. You've got to recognize it for what it is: crumbs."

"The tricky thing is you don't know they're crumbs...until you know. You take the crumbs and you're so grateful because you don't know what cake is. Cake is so far from your understanding of what is possible. It's taken me forever to figure this out. I don't think I've known what it is to be loved by someone, but..." I pause here. My eyes once again get teary, but these are good tears. "You've taught me how to be loved. I know, I know, you're going to tell me to shut up, but I need to tell you this. This whole time, through all the shit I've been through, you've supported me and been there. You've talked to me and cried with me. Taught me how to drill shit."

"I put together your furniture."

"You put together my furniture. And not once, not one time did I ever feel like I had to be someone else around you. Someone better. I never felt like I was asking too much."

"Well, you've been there for me too. I don't know how I'd have made it through this last year without you. Seriously."

"Really?"

"Yes, really." Erin smiles wide. "I guess what we are both saying is that we're the love story here."

I nod. "We are."

"Good, because men fucking exhaust me, and if I have to live a boring and trauma-free life, I'd like to do it with you."

"I have a feeling, if we stay in this together, it's not going to be so boring," I say.

Erin nods. “Fuck yeah. Our lives? They’re going to be beautiful.”

“Maybe our lives already are.”

We don’t high-five, but there’s a little moment where we don’t say anything.

Because we don’t need to.

The server delivers our pasta. Mine is piled high with wild mushrooms. Erin’s has three different kinds of meat. We clink our cocktails and say cheers. We talk about normal, everyday things.

When we’re done with our pasta, Erin gives me another smile, and then leans in as if sharing a wild and wicked secret. “I’m going to ask the chef if they can whip us up some waffles. We deserve it,” she says.

She’s right.

We do.

# Author's Note

It feels like I should write an epilogue here, where I tie everything up and everything feels good and cozy. Real lives don't have epilogues though. You just have another day. Some things resolve, some things don't.

My mom still calls me to tell me how great her life with Frank is. She still checks to see when we can get together and if she can see the kids. I'm still firm on my boundaries on not seeing her yet. Not until I'm a little steadier in my own life and this new way of living.

I am steadier. Every day, more so.

Matthew comes over every now and then to take the dogs for a weekend. We chat. Small talk. It's okay. I don't think we've resolved our hurt and anger toward each other, but there seems to be a gentle acceptance there. We did the best we could. He seems happy. He seems okay.

I learn to set some boundaries with dating. I keep seeing the man who reminds me of a lumberjack. I've always had a thing for Paul Bunyan, so this is exciting to me. He is different from anyone I've dated, and that is a comfort. When we met, we stood awkwardly on the sidewalk waiting to get into the restaurant and I said, "Hi, I'm Tanya." I held out my hand. He went in for the hug, and later we will laugh when he tells me, "Man, I almost blew it with that hug. I didn't realize you weren't a hugger."

By the time he tells me that, I will like hugging him. I will love hugging him. He will love hugging me back.

Erin and I still walk. We talk on the phone every day. And there are more things that happen to us, because that is life. Life happens. There is drama and illness and health and heartache. She breaks up with her husband for good. We sign her up on a dating app and it is wild and hilarious, and also a little bit sad. She is learning how to date. She stops smoking, and she still swears like a sailor. She is still angry.

We eat a lot of brownies together.

I am learning how to be in a healthy relationship. How to communicate my wants and needs, and how to be firm in what, and who, I need in my life.

My kids live with me full time. We are all adjusting to life in the now and the life to come: pronouns, identities, college, leaving home. The kids have struggles. They're normal kids, and their struggles are part of growing up and growing into who they are. There is a hearing set for child support next month. Their dad will attend via Zoom. He won't be back from his hike for another two months. I don't know what the outcome of the hearing will be, but I'm proud of myself for putting this in motion.

I still narrate, but there seem to be more thrillers and mysteries in my queue than romances. It doesn't matter what book I perform, I love the stories, the lives I get to step into.

I keep writing. My blog, my tiny poems, a book, this memoir. I write because it helps me understand the world and it feeds my soul. And I hope that my words will reach out and connect with someone who needs to hear them.

I spend time with my lumberjack. Not just Tuesdays, but weekends too. We hike together, forage deep in the woods in Michigan. We drive around, looking for oyster mushrooms clinging to oak trees, or side stands of fresh sweet corn, or wild asparagus, his warm hand on my bony knee. We laugh a lot. We touch and kiss and love. We are grateful for each other. We are grateful for all the things we've been through because it somehow led us to each other.

I don't know if this relationship will last forever, but I don't need to know. I am comfortable in the now.

I don't know what happens to Ryan. I suspect he keeps living the way he's always lived. I hope he becomes more honest with women he sees so they can make a choice about the kind of relationship they are involved with. I like to think that's what happens, but I'm doubtful.

I talk to my friends, my family. I reach out. I garden. I grow mushrooms in my backyard. I play with my dogs. I make fresh jam from mulberries and farm fresh strawberries.

I live my life.

Boldly. Wildly. Without apologizing.

When I think back on these last three years of starting over again, mostly, I am grateful. Not for the pain...no one wants that, but the experiences that have made me wiser. And I am grateful for my friendship with Erin, which is the love story I wanted and didn't know I was experiencing. For a long time, I did not know how to love or how to be loved, but she helped me to learn.

I am still learning.

What I know now is that I was never a Tuesday Girl. I thought I was less than, and it was that thought that held me back.

You are not a Tuesday girl either. You have worth. You are meant to be loved.

I'm sitting by a lake writing these last words. There are houses wrapped around the lake and I think of all the people living inside those houses, or walking city streets, or in apartments, cabins, condos, whatever. We all have stories. We all struggle. We learn. We do the best we can. And every day, we turn the page of our own story and start anew.

That's the magic of living.

Here's to turning the page.

Here's to walking the next mile.

And like Erin says, "Here's to living your big fucking beautiful life."

# About the Author

If you've read The Tuesday Girl, then you know all about Tanya. She's a narrator, a mom, and a writer who lives in Grand Rapids, Michigan with her two teenagers and two pups. Follow her on social media at Facebook, Instagram, and Threads.

Made in United States
Orlando, FL
26 September 2023